ESSENTIAL SQA EXAM PRACTICE

NATIONAL 5 COMPUTING SCIENCE

Practice Questions & Exam Papers

QUESTIONS & PAPERS

Practise **40+ multi-part questions** covering every topic

Complete **2 practice papers** that mirror the real SQA exams

Lesley Russell

Boost

Hodder Gibson
AN HACHETTE UK COMPANY

Although every effort has been made to ensure that website addresses are correct at time of going to press, Hodder Gibson cannot be held responsible for the content of any website mentioned in this book. It is sometimes possible to find a relocated webpage by typing in the address of the home page for a website in the URL window of your browser.

Hachette UK's policy is to use papers that are natural, renewable and recyclable products and made from wood grown in well-managed forests and other controlled sources. The logging and manufacturing processes are expected to conform to the environmental regulations of the country of origin.

Orders: please contact Hachette UK Distribution, Hely Hutchinson Centre, Milton Road, Didcot, Oxfordshire, OX11 7HH.
Telephone: +44 (0)1235 827827. Email: education@hachette.co.uk. Lines are open from 9 a.m. to 5 p.m., Monday to Friday. You can also order through our website: www.hoddereducation.co.uk. If you have queries or questions that aren't about an order, you can contact us at hoddergibson@hodder.co.uk.

© Lesley Russell 2021

First published in 2021 by

Hodder Gibson, an imprint of Hodder Education

An Hachette UK Company

50 Frederick Street

Edinburgh, EH2 1EX

Impression number   5   4

Year   2025 2024

Illustrations by Aptara Inc.

Typeset in India by Aptara Inc.

Printed and bound by Ashford Colour Press Ltd

A catalogue record for this title is available from the British Library.
ISBN: 978 1 3983 1822 9

SCOTLAND EXCEL

We are an approved supplier on the Scotland Excel framework.

Find us on your school's procurement system as *Hachette UK Distribution Ltd* or *Hodder & Stoughton Limited t/a Hodder Education.*

CONTENTS

INTRODUCTION

National 5 Computing Science

How to use this book

The purpose of this book is to provide you with focused exam practice. The first part of the book contains practice questions, divided into the two question types that you will see in the question paper, together with advice on answering each type of question. The first part is split across the four areas of study: Software design and development, Computer systems, Database design and development, and Web design and development. This part has a student margin stating the content being assessed in that question.

The second part of this book contains two complete question papers designed to mimic closely the question paper you will face. The book contains answer guides as well as a revision grid that allows you to target a specific area of content should you require further practice on a specific topic.

This book can be used in two ways:

1 You can complete a practice question using your notes and books. The questions are divided into areas of study in Part 1 of the book so are ideal for doing this. Try the question first, and then refer to the answer guidelines to ensure you have sufficient detail to gain all the available marks. If you are unable to answer a question, or discover your answer was not to the required standard, you should refer to your notes and books.

2 You can complete an entire practice paper under examination conditions, without reference to books or notes, and then mark your answers using the answer guidelines provided. The two complete papers in Part 2 of the book are ideal for doing this. This will give you a clear indication of the level at which you are currently working and enable you to target any areas of content in which you need to improve.

The course

Prerequisite knowledge

Before sitting this course, it is expected that you will have achieved the fourth curriculum level or the National 4 Computing Science course or have the equivalent computing knowledge and experience.

The Assignment

The Assignment will be worth 50 marks. This will be combined with a 110 mark question paper to give a total of 160 available marks.

The Assignment will have 25 marks assigned to Software design and development, 10–15 marks assigned to Database design and development and 10–15 marks assigned to Web design and development. The Assignment does not assess Computer systems at all and all assessment of this area of study will take place through the question paper.

The Assignment will require you to show your understanding and skills in the following areas:

▶ Analysis of a problem – 5 marks
▶ Design of a solution – 5 marks
▶ Implementation of a solution – 30 marks
▶ Testing a solution – 5 marks
▶ Evaluation of a solution – 5 marks

The question paper

The question paper will assess your problem-solving ability, making reference to technical knowledge on the areas stated within the Course Specification. The Course Specification document can be accessed for free from the National 5 Computing Science section of the SQA website. This document has a number of appendices designed to clarify the content and it is advised that all candidates study these to ensure understanding of the key points that they cover.

The current format of the question paper consists of 110 marks.

Section 1 will consist of individual problem-solving questions and is worth a total of 25 marks.

Section 2 will consist of longer, scenario-based problem-solving questions and is worth a total of 85 marks.

The question paper assesses your understanding and skills in the following areas of content:

▶ Software design and development (approximately 40%)
▶ Computer systems (approximately 10%)
▶ Database design and development (approximately 25%)
▶ Web design and development (approximately 25%)

The question paper will require you to show your understanding and skills in the following areas:

▶ Analysis of a problem (approximately 5%)
▶ Design of a solution (approximately 30%)
▶ Implementation of a solution (approximately 40%)
▶ Testing a solution (approximately 10%)
▶ Evaluation of a solution (approximately 5%)
▶ Application of knowledge in computer systems (approximately 10%)

Hints and tips

Below is a list of hints and tips that will help you in your National 5 Computing Science SQA examination paper:

▶ Make sure you read each question carefully. The detail in the question sets the scene for the problem to be solved.
▶ Refer to the situation described in the question. The papers are designed to test how a candidate applies their knowledge to a situation.
▶ Use technical terms. A National 5 level answer will require certain terms from the course to be used. Download the Course Specification document from the SQA website to help.
▶ No marks will be given for repeating information given in the question. You can and should refer to the question, but build on that with the points you wish to make in order to gain the marks.
▶ Include as much detail as you can. As you will see from the answer guidelines, many questions have multiple possible answers. If a marker deems that you lack enough technical detail to give you a mark on one point, they can still give you the mark for a separate fully explained point. As much as possible, SQA markers undertake positive marking. This means that if a question is worth 2 marks, and a candidate makes one wrong point and two correct points, they will be awarded the 2 marks.
▶ When answering questions involving calculations, show all your working. If you make a small mistake under pressure, you might still gain some of the available marks.
▶ Attempt all questions. Leaving an answer blank means you will definitely receive no marks for it.
▶ Some candidates will have used programming languages where arrays are indexed beginning with element[1]. In SQA exams, arrays are indexed from zero, not 1.

Regular revision from the outset of the course is the best way to ensure you can recall the full detail required. Set aside time each week for this.

Remember sometimes your biggest resource is people. Speak to your teacher about any concerns that you have, support your classmates and enjoy their support in return. Good luck realising your potential in National 5 Computing Science.

KEY SKILLS GRID

Key area	Practice Questions Section 1	Section 2	Paper 1 Section 1	Section 2	Paper 2 Section 1	Section 2
Software design and development						
Development methodologies	1					
Analysis	2	1a		11a,15d		16a
Design	3	1b, 2a, 3a, 3b, 4d, 5a	5, 6a	11b, 14a, 15e	12	13a, 13f
Implementation (data types and structures)	4, 5	4a		17a		13c, 16bi, 16bii
Implementation (computational constructs)	6, 7	1c, 1d, 2b, 2c, 3ei, 4b, 4c, 5b		11di,14bi, 14bii,14c, 17bii,17biii	3a, 9a	13b, 13e, 16d
Implementation (algorithm specification)		1e, 5c		11c, 14biii		13d, 16c
Testing	8, 9, 10	2d, 3c, 3d, 3eii	3c, 6b	14d,17bi,17c	5b, 9b	13g, 16e
Evaluation	11	2d, 3eiii			7	
Computer systems						
Data representation	1, 2, 3, 4	2a, 2b, 2c, 2d	1, 3a, 3b	11dii, 12ei, 16a	1	15ci, 16bii
Computer structure	5, 6	2e, 2f, 2g	10b		3b, 5a, 11	
Environmental impact	7					18g
Security risks and precautions	8, 9	1a, 1b	2c			
Database design and development						
Analysis	1			13a		18di
Design	2, 3, 4, 5	1a, 1b, 1c, 1d, 2a		13b, 13c, 13d, 15a	2, 6, 10	14a, 14b, 14ci, 18a, 18b, 18c
Implementation	6	2bi, 2c, 2d, 2e, 2fii, 3a, 3b	4, 8	15c		14cii,14ciii, 18dii
Testing		2bii, 2fi	10a	15b		18e
Evaluation						18f
Web design and development						
Analysis	1	2a				15a
Design	2	1a, 2b, 2d	2a, 7	12a, 12eii, 12g, 12h, 16b		15b, 15cii, 15d, 15eiii, 17d
Implementation (CSS)	7, 8	1b, 2e, 3a, 3b		16c, 16di, 16dii	4	15f, 17a, 17b, 17f
Implementation (HTML)	3, 4, 5, 6	1c, 1d, 1e, 1g, 2c, 2f	9	12b, 12d, 12g		15ei, 15eii, 17e
Implementation (JavaScript)		3c, 3d		12f		17ci
Testing		1f, 3e		12c	8	17cii
Evaluation	9		2b			17g
Total marks	/68	/152	/25	/85	/25	/85

Section 1 questions

>> HOW TO ANSWER

Section 1 in the question paper contains a number of questions that have short, restricted responses. The questions will be related to one of the four main areas of study – Software design and development, Computer systems, Database design and development, or Web design and development. They may be single questions or split into two parts. Questions are likely to be of 'C' or 'B' level of difficulty, where you have to recall knowledge and terminology and apply it to fairly straightforward problem-solving situations.

Top Tip!

Look for the command words such as Identify, State, Write, Describe, Complete, Explain. If a question says 'State', a short answer is often sufficient. If a question says 'Identify' then you have to name something specific using the correct terminology or find the answer in the stem of the question or a diagram. 'Describe' means you need to set out the characteristics of something. 'Explain' will involve giving reasons or the purposes of something.

MARKS	STUDENT MARGIN

Software design and development

Questions covering all the stages of an iterative development process. Implementation questions require reading, understanding, explaining and writing code.

1 The software development process is iterative. Explain how the word iterative applies to this process.

    MARKS: 1 — STUDENT MARGIN: Development methodologies

2 Josef is making a kite. He uses two canes for the main struts. He decides to write a program to work out how much paper is needed to make the sail.
Complete the analysis of the problem by identifying the inputs and outputs.

    MARKS: 2 — STUDENT MARGIN: Analysis

Input	
Process	Work out area of sail by multiplying length of cane 1 by length of cane 2 and halving the answer
Output	

Hint!

Read the scenario carefully. Work out the inputs and outputs by considering the values referred to in the stem of the question or the process description.

		MARKS	STUDENT MARGIN

3 Richard is creating a program to enable customers to obtain a price for buying turf. The user needs to enter the area to be turfed and whether they want to add an extra 5% to ensure coverage.

The program determines the cost per m², as customers benefit from cheaper prices for larger projects. This value and the final overall price should both be displayed in the customer's quote.

Using the information above, design a user interface for the program.

MARKS: 4 — **Design**

Top Tip!

Work out the inputs and outputs before you start to sketch a possible screen layout. In your user interface design include instructions for the user as well as spaces for values to be entered so they know what values have to go in each place. Make sure you also label sections to display the outputs.

4 A program stores the names of the patron saints of 50 different countries.

State the data structure and data type that will be required to store the 50 names.

MARKS: 2 — **Implementation (data types and structures)**

Hint!

Whenever a list of items of the same data type are stored, an array data structure should be used. You need to give the data type for the items in the list as well – integer, real, character, string or Boolean.

5 A cinema requires a program to work out the total cost of tickets ordered by a customer based on three inputs:
- SeatType – for example: standard or recliner
- TicketPrice – for example: 3.99 or 5.50
- QuantityOrdered – for example: 4

State the data type of each variable.

MARKS: 3 — **Implementation (data types and structures)**

Top Tip!

There are several data types that you should be able to use:
- character
- string
- numeric (integer and real)
- Boolean

6 The program code below uses a loop to traverse the items of an array.

MARKS: 3 — **Implementation (computational constructs)**

```
Line 1 SET fruits TO ["apple", "orange", "banana", "cherry",
       "grape"]
Line 2 FOR index FROM 0 TO 4 DO
Line 3 _____
Line 4 END FOR
```

MARKS | STUDENT MARGIN

Using a programming language of your choice, complete Line 3 so the following output is given when the program is tested.

Fruit 1 is called apple

Fruit 2 is called orange

Fruit 3 is called banana

Fruit 4 is called cherry

Fruit 5 is called grape

 Hint!

Write code in the programming language you used during your course. You must refer to the code given in the question to use the correct variable names. You need to use the loop counter variable to traverse the array.

7 This program allows users to spin the wheel to pick one of the six activities to do.

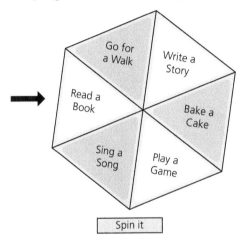

Spin it

Line 20 `DECLARE activityList INITIALLY [ "Write a Story","Bake a Cake","Play a Game","Sing a Song","Read a Book","Go for a Walk" ]`

Line 21 `<use a pre-defined function to pick an activity from the list>`

State the predefined function and a parameter that could be used in Line 21.

2 | Implementation (computational constructs)

Top Tip!

Functions are sections of code used to return a single value to a variable. There are three predefined functions you should be able to describe and implement:
- random
- round
- length

A parameter is information that the function needs to be able to work properly.

	MARKS	STUDENT MARGIN

8 A program is used to validate percentages scored by pupils in a test. The following test data is used:

Normal: 34   57   85

Extreme: 0   100

State two possible numeric values for exceptional data.

> **Hint!**
>
> Exceptional data values are values that would not be accepted by the program.

MARKS: 2 — STUDENT MARGIN: Testing

9 A delivery company uses a program to work out the category of a parcel.

...

```
Line 15 RECEIVE parcelweight FROM <scales>
Line 16 RECEIVE parcellength FROM KEYBOARD
Line 17 IF (parcelweight>=1 AND parcelweight<=20) AND
        NOT(parcellength>40) THEN
Line 18   SET category TO <small>
Line 19 ELSE
Line 20   SET category TO <medium>
Line 21 END IF
```

...

State one normal test data value for parcelweight and one normal test data value for parcellength that will set the category to small.

> **Hint!**
>
> Use the conditions in Line 17 to work out appropriate values.

MARKS: 2 — STUDENT MARGIN: Testing

10 Imran has written a program to count how many people are old enough to vote in a general election. You have to be at least 18 years old to be eligible to vote. He tests the program with the following data:

Name	Age
Joe	18
Jez	19
Jamillah	17
Jadzia	19

The following output is produced: 'The number of people old enough to vote is 2'

Explain why Imran's program must contain a logic error.

MARKS: 2 — STUDENT MARGIN: Testing

> **Top Tip!**
>
> There are three types of errors you should be able to describe and identify:
> - syntax error
> - execution error
> - logic error

	MARKS	STUDENT MARGIN

11 A program is written to generate a five-digit code by combining five random numbers. Each digit must be unique within the code.

```
Line 1  DECLARE code AS INTEGER INITIALLY 0
Line 2  <declare five variables as integers, one for each
        digit>
...
Line 8  SET digit1 TO <random number between 0 and 9>
Line 9  SET digit2 TO <random number between 0 and 9>
Line 10 SET digit3 TO <random number between 0 and 9>
Line 11 SET digit4 TO <random number between 0 and 9>
Line 12 SET digit5 TO <random number between 0 and 9>
Line 13 SET code TO digit1 + digit2 + digit3 + digit4 + digit5
Line 14 SEND code TO DISPLAY
```

a) When evaluating this code, it is found that it does not produce the expected output. Explain why this code is not fit for purpose.

Marks: 1 — Student Margin: Evaluation

b) During evaluation it is also suggested that more efficient use of programming constructs could have been used. Identify one way this code could have been written using a more efficient construct.

Marks: 1

Computer systems

Questions about data representation, basic computer architecture, the environmental impact of the energy use of computing systems and security precautions that can be taken to protect computer systems.

1 Convert the 8-bit binary number 10101101 into denary.

Marks: 1 — Student Margin: Data representation

> **Hint!**
>
> Columns are labelled from the right as units and doubling as they move to the left
>
> | 128 | 64 | 32 | 16 | 8 | 4 | 2 | 1 |
> |---|---|---|---|---|---|---|---|
> | 1 | 0 | 1 | 0 | 1 | 1 | 0 | 1 |

2 Convert the decimal number 52 into 8-bit binary.

Marks: 1 — Student Margin: Data representation

> **Hint!**
>
> Don't forget to give leading zeros to ensure there are 8 bits

3 The value 23 428.49 would be stored in a computer system using floating-point representation as $0.234\,284\,9 \times 10^5$.
Identify the mantissa and the exponent.

Marks: 2 — Student Margin: Data representation

4 A digital safety deposit box uses a seven-character code to open it. State the number of bits required to store the code.

Marks: 1 — Student Margin: Data representation

> **Hint!**
>
> Extended ASCII uses 8 bits for each character.

	MARKS	STUDENT MARGIN

5 State the part of the processor that compares the values in a conditional statement.

1 — Computer structure

Top Tip!

You need to know the basic computer architecture components and how they are linked together – processor (registers, ALU, control unit), memory locations and buses (data bus, address bus).

6 Explain how a computer system identifies each memory location so that data can be retrieved.

1 — Computer structure

7 Describe one way that a company could reduce the energy their computer systems use.

1 — Environmental impact

8 A school database contains personal data about pupils and teachers. State one precaution that could be taken to prevent hackers accessing the database.

1 — Security precautions

9 Teachers can log into the school administration database from home to access pupil reports. Describe how encryption could be used to keep data secure during transmission.

1 — Security precautions

Database design and development

Questions about all the stages of developing database systems. This includes working out requirements of a database, designing entities and their attributes, creating queries in SQL and testing and evaluating solutions. The questions are usually set in a scenario.

1 A company wants to create a database to store details of employees. Initially, it is suggested that the following items of data are stored: EmployeeID, forename, surname, address and town.

2 — Analysis

The database developers ask some of the administrators of the company what they would like to see in the database.

One supervisor says he wants to be able to produce a list of staff in alphabetical order. One department head says she wants to produce lists of employees in the sales department. A payroll administrator says he wants to get lists of employees who are on paygrade 5.
Describe a problem with the proposed database functionality by referring to the end-user requirements.

Top Tip!

You need to know about end-user requirements – the tasks the users expect to be able to do using the database. You also need to know about functional requirements – the processes the system has to perform and the information it has to contain to be able to carry out its functions.

Read the question carefully to establish what the end users want to do, checking whether the system is able to perform these activities.

MARKS   **STUDENT MARGIN**

2 When using some databases, businesses have to consider the implications of the General Data Protection Regulation (GDPR). Describe two implications for a business using a database that contains personal information. — **2** — Design

3 A database is designed to store information about pupils and their class in primary school. The attributes of each entity are shown below. — Design

Entity: Pupil

pupilID	P101
firstname	Pat
lastname	Black
group	7A

Entity: Class

group	7A
teacher	Ms Jay
room	4

a) Identify the primary and foreign keys in each entity. — **3**

b) Describe the relationship that exists between the two tables. — **1**

4 A factory has four departments called Purchasing, Production, Sales and Despatch. The company is planning to create a database to store information about factory employees. — **3** — Design

Entity: Employee

Attribute Name	Key	Type	Size	Required	Validation
employeeID	A	Text	9	Yes	length=9
firstName		Text	20	Yes	
lastName		Text	20	Yes	
department		Text	20	Yes	B
jobTitle		Text	20	Yes	
yearAppointed		C		No	

State the missing information for A, B and C to complete the data dictionary.

Top Tip!

You need to know how data dictionaries are used, as well as what is included in them. It is unlikely that you will be asked to design a whole data dictionary.

MARKS	STUDENT MARGIN
3	Design

5 A database about football teams stores the following details
- team name
- city
- stadium
- year formed
- capacity
- average ticket price

Jordan is trying to find out which teams in Glasgow were formed before 1910 and wants a list of the team names along with their stadium and average ticket price. These should be arranged with the cheapest average ticket price at the top.

Complete the query design to find all the matching teams.

Top Tip!

To design a query, always read the question carefully before you answer. It is useful to highlight the search criteria and sort order in the question. The 'things to find' help you work out the search criteria and the way the data is to be arranged is the sort order.

Field(s)	team name, stadium, average ticket price
Table(s)	Teams
Search criteria	
Sort order	

6 The sorted output below was produced by running a query in a database.

lastName	department
Adams	Sales
Bradley	Sales
Jimenez	Sales
Wallace	Sales
Jones	Purchasing
Omar	Purchasing
Thorpe	Purchasing
Brown	Production
Caesar	Production
Lopinski	Production
Watkins	Production
Adams	Despatch
James	Despatch
McLeod	Despatch

Top Tip!

It is common at this level to be asked about sorting on more than one field. It is usually fairly easy to spot one column that has been arranged in order, but at National 5 always check to see if there is a second column that has also been sorted.

2	Implementation

Complete the SQL statement used to produce this output.

```
SELECT lastName, department
FROM Employee
ORDER BY _____
```

MARKS	STUDENT MARGIN

Web design and development

Questions about all the stages of developing websites. This includes working out requirements for a website, designing webpages and understanding media content, creating webpages using HTML, CSS and JavaScript and testing and evaluating solutions. The questions are usually set in a scenario.

1 Name the stage of the software development process when the end-user and functional requirements of a website are identified.

1	Analysis

2 Trndi Fashion wants to create a new home page for their website. They require the company logo just below the company name which should be centred at the top of the page. Under the logo but stretching the width of the page, they want a paragraph introducing the company. They would also like a bulleted list of links to the following sections: Designers, Products and Materials positioned below the introduction.

Draw a wireframe to illustrate the proposed user interface.

4	Design

Top Tip!

A wireframe is used to plan the user interface for each page on a website. Each wireframe indicates the intended layout of the page and shows the position of all text elements on the page, any media elements and the intended position of all hyperlinks on the page.

3 Add HTML p, a and head opening and closing elements to complete the code below.

2	Implementation (HTML)

Top Tip!

There is a wide range of HTML elements you must be able to use: head, title, body, heading, paragraph, DIV, link, anchor, IMG, audio, video, lists — ol, ul and li.

```
<html>
<_____>
<title>Creating a Website</title>
<_____>
<body>
<h1>Website heading</h1>
<_____>The first section of text goes in here<_____>
<_____ href="http://w3schools.com"> Click here for help
with HTML<_____>
</body>
</html>
```

		MARKS	STUDENT MARGIN

4 Sketch the output from the following HTML code:

```
<ol>
<li>Contents</li>
<li>Introduction</li>
<li>Revision</li>
<li>Test</li>
</ol>
```

MARKS: 2 — Implementation (HTML)

> **Hint!**
>
> <ol> and <ul> can both be used for lists in HTML. <ol> is short for ordered lists meaning the list items are placed in order …1, 2, 3 or a, b, c etc.
>
> <ul> is short for unordered list meaning the list items are displayed without ordering, using bullet points or other markers.

5 The hyperlink below is used to take visitors using a book shop website to a book publisher website.

```
<a href ="http://www.hoddergibson.co.uk/">Hodder Gibson website</a>
```

Identify the type of addressing used in this hyperlink.

MARKS: 1 — Implementation (HMTL)

> **Hint!**
>
> Links with absolute addresses point directly to a specific location to access. They include all information needed for the browser to locate the file, including the server address, path and filename.
>
> Relative addresses point to a location in the same directory on the same server as the source. They contain only the path and filename.

6 The address of a website is: www.romeholidays.co.uk/home.html.

A folder called pix is created in the same directory as the home page. Graphics to be used on the home page are placed in the folder.

Write the HTML to display a photo of the city, with the filename rome.jpg on the home.html page.

MARKS: 2 — Implementation (HTML)

7 The following CSS rule is used to style part of a webpage:

```
.subject{background-color:red;}
```

Identify the type of selector used above.

MARKS: 1 — Implementation (CSS)

> **Top Tip!**
>
> A CSS selector is used to select the HTML elements to be formatted.
>
> A class selector is used to format elements with a class attribute. Many HTML elements can share the same class so a single CSS rule can be used to style many elements.
>
> The id selector is used to format HTML elements with an id attribute. There cannot be more than one element on a page with the same id.

	MARKS	STUDENT MARGIN
	2	Implementation (CSS)
	1	Evaluation

8 The following code is part of a webpage.

```
...
<style>
#heading {background-color:white;color:black;}
.subheading {background-color:black;color:white;}
</style>
...
<p id="heading">Computing</p>
<p class="subheading">Contents</p>
<p class="subheading">Intro</p>
<p class="subheading">Revision</p>
<p class="subheading">Test</p>
...
```

Explain why some of the paragraphs have an id attribute and others have a class attribute.

9 A debating society wants a website to provide information about the society and the dates of upcoming debates. The completed home page is shown below.

Debating Society

You've been given 15 minutes to build a convincing argument for something you know nothing about...Go!

Our debating society will help develop you public speaking skills, build your confidence, meet some great people and have fun.

This is the place to find out more information about the society and aspects of debating.

- Who We Are
- Training Workshops
- Membership

Evaluate the website in terms of its fitness for purpose.

> **Hint!**
>
> Evaluation of a website is done by comparing the finished product with the end-user and functional requirements established during the analysis stage.

Section 2 questions

>> HOW TO ANSWER

In Section 2 the questions consist of several longer problem-solving questions split into many parts. Each question will relate in the main part to one of three of the areas of study. There are no questions that relate in whole to Computer systems. However, such questions are integrated into the questions on the three other topics. In the question paper, 30% of the questions will be of A-level difficulty and these are likely to be in this section. These questions often involve combining several steps to solve problems, writing code for complex scenarios or explaining complex sets of instructions.

Each question sets out a scenario or situation at the beginning which continues to apply for all parts of that question. Each part may add new information to build on that given previously. Make sure you relate your answers to the scenario or situation in the question.

In this section you really need to think about the scenarios and apply your knowledge to the problems set.

Top Tip!

Download the Course Specification document from the SQA website and use it as a checklist for revision topics. It will help you to recognise the terminology used in the question paper. It will also help you to clarify what kind of response is expected in some questions. For example, if you are asked to identify a design technique for programming, then there are only three possible answers and they are listed in the document. Similarly, if you are asked to write a program design then you should use one of these three techniques.

	MARKS	STUDENT MARGIN

Software design and development

Longer questions with many parts, each part of a question being set within the same scenario. You need to read and explain complex designs and programs and apply your knowledge of programming constructs to the scenarios.

1   Alison is doing a million step challenge. She wears a device to count the number of steps she does and writes this down for each day during the month of May. On 31 May, she types the number of steps she took each day into a program which will tell her whether she reached the 1 000 000 step target or not. The number of steps must be a whole number more than or equal to zero.

   a)   Analyse the problem and identify all the inputs, processes and outputs.

   3   Analysis

Hint!

Read the scenario carefully, highlighting the values to be entered, the actions the program has to carry out and the results to be produced. Processes are sometimes not specified explicitly – you can work them out by considering what is done to the inputs to produce the outputs.

MARKS   STUDENT MARGIN

Here is the design for the program.

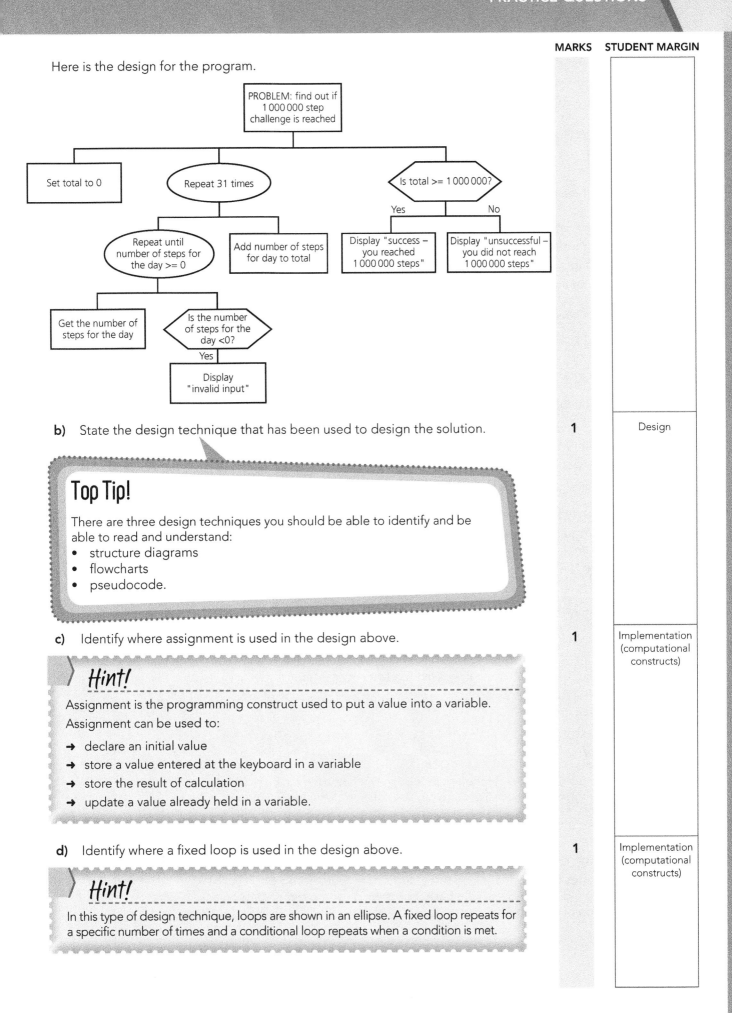

b) State the design technique that has been used to design the solution.

1   Design

Top Tip!

There are three design techniques you should be able to identify and be able to read and understand:
- structure diagrams
- flowcharts
- pseudocode.

c) Identify where assignment is used in the design above.

1   Implementation (computational constructs)

Hint!

Assignment is the programming construct used to put a value into a variable.

Assignment can be used to:

→ declare an initial value

→ store a value entered at the keyboard in a variable

→ store the result of calculation

→ update a value already held in a variable.

d) Identify where a fixed loop is used in the design above.

1   Implementation (computational constructs)

Hint!

In this type of design technique, loops are shown in an ellipse. A fixed loop repeats for a specific number of times and a conditional loop repeats when a condition is met.

	MARKS	STUDENT MARGIN

e) State the standard algorithm used to:

  (i) check the number of steps entered is greater than 0

  (ii) add the number of days to the total.

> **MARKS:** 2
>
> **STUDENT MARGIN:** Implementation (algorithm specification)

Top Tip!

There are three standard algorithms that you should be able to recognise and code

- input validation
- running total within loop
- traversing a 1-D array

They may be adapted to suit specific problems.

2 Wiktoria designs a program to display the odd numbers less than 6.

a) Algorithm

  1. Initially store 1 in variable called number

  2. Repeat until number is more than 6

  3.   Add 2 to number

  4.   Display number

  5. End loop

State the design technique that has been used above.

> **MARKS:** 1
>
> **STUDENT MARGIN:** Design

b) State which type of loop is used in the design above.

> **MARKS:** 1
>
> **STUDENT MARGIN:** Implementation (computational constructs)

c) Using a programming language of your choice, show how 'add 2 to number' would be implemented.

> **MARKS:** 2
>
> **STUDENT MARGIN:** Implementation (computational constructs)

Hint!

You must use the variable names referred to in the question or diagram. Make sure you assign the result to the appropriate variable.

d) After coding her design accurately, Wiktoria tests her program.

Explain whether Wiktoria's program is fit for purpose, giving a reason for your answer.

> **MARKS:** 2
>
> **STUDENT MARGIN:** Testing/ Evaluation

Hint!

Evaluating a program is fit for purpose is done by comparing the purpose of the program with the actual output to see if the requirements have been met.

3 Billy is organising a 'hook a duck' stall for a school summer fayre.

The game involves the player hooking three ducks at random from a pool. Each duck has a single digit number on the base. Prizes are awarded depending on the combination of the numbers.

The design for the game is shown below.

	MARKS	STUDENT MARGIN

a) State the design technique that has been used. — 1 — Design

b) Explain why a loop is shown in the design. — 1 — Design

c) Write down a set of test data that will result in the following prizes being awarded. — 2 — Testing

   (i) First prize awarded.

   (ii) Second prize awarded.

d) Describe the expected result of the following ducks being hooked. — 2 — Testing

   ① ② ②

e) Billy is unsure how many winning combinations exist and writes a program to work this out.

Top Tip!

In the exam paper, program code is written in SQA reference language. Some lines use elision <...> which allows the inclusion of steps that have not been fully worked out yet.

```
Line 1    <initialise variables>
...
Line 10   <repeat for each possible combination numbers
          from 1 to 9>
Line 11    SET totalCombos TO totalCombos +1
Line 12    IF (duck1=duck2) AND (duck2=duck3) THEN
Line 13      SET threeSame TO threeSame +1
Line 14    END IF
```

		MARKS	STUDENT MARGIN

```
Line 15    IF duck1+duck2+duck3<10 THEN
Line 16      SET sumTen TO sumTen +1
Line 17    END IF
Line 18    IF _____ THEN
Line 19      SET twoSame TO twoSame +1
Line 20    END IF
Line 21    <end loop>
```

(i) Using a programming language of your choice, complete Line 18.

4 — Implementation (computational constructs)

> **Hint!**
>
> Look back at the flowchart to see the criteria for third prize.

(ii) The value in the totalCombos variable after the program is run is 729. State the name of the variable assigned the number of first prize combinations.

1 — Testing

(iii) The program includes meaningful variable names and indentation to improve readability.

Describe one other technique used in programming to improve readability. Explain how it could be used in the program above.

2 — Evaluation

> **Top Tip!**
>
> There are four techniques you should know to improve readability – often you will be asked to apply this knowledge to a given program and not just recall the techniques.

4 Members of a club are asked to vote for one of three options A, B or C. A program is being designed to count the votes to find the most popular option.

The design is shown below.

Algorithm

1. Initialise variables
2. For each vote cast
3. Count votes for each option
4. End loop
5. Check for most popular option
6. Display result of voting

Refinement

1.1 votes are A,B,C,A,A,B,C,A,B,A,C,B,A,C,B,A
1.2 totalA is 0
1.3 totalB is 0
1.4 totalC is 0

a) State the data structure and data type that will be required to implement the list of votes.

2 — Implementation (data types and structures)

b) Name the predefined function and its parameter that can be used during implementation to find out how many votes are cast.

2 — Implementation (computational constructs)

c) Identify the type of loop required at Step 2.

1 — Implementation (computational constructs)

d) Using a design technique of your choice, refine Step 3.

4 — Design

5   Jackie is paid £8 per hour. Overtime hours are paid at 1.5 times the normal rate per hour. For weekend work the normal hourly rate is doubled.
Each week, Jackie records the hours worked in a time sheet like the one below.

Employee name	Jackie
Rate per hour (£)	8.00
Normal hours	40
Overtime hours	3
Weekend hours	8

A program is used to calculate earnings.

...

```
Line 10 DECLARE rate AS REAL INITIALLY 8.00
Line 11 DECLARE weeklypay AS REAL INITIALLY 0.00
...
Line 22 RECEIVE hours FROM KEYBOARD
Line 23 RECEIVE overtime FROM KEYBOARD
Line 24 RECEIVE weekend FROM KEYBOARD
...
```

a)   Explain why the variable called rate has been declared as a real data type.

b)   Using a programming language of your choice, write the code to calculate the weekly pay for an employee.

c)   The pay earned each week during a month is stored in an array.

```
Line 31 DECLARE julyPay INITIALLY [ 520.00, 502.00,
        480.00, 545.00 ]
Line 32 DECLARE total INITIALLY 0.00
Line 33 FOR number FROM 0 TO 3 DO
Line 34 _____
Line 35 END FOR
```

Using a programming language of your choice, complete the code to find the total earned.

MARKS: 1 — Design
4 — Implementation (computational constructs)
3 — Implementation (algorithm specification)

Computer systems

Section 2 questions are not on the topic of Computer systems alone. Instead, questions from the other topics will have one or two parts addressing this area of study.

1   A website offers customers the opportunity to order and pay for goods online.

a)   The website uses encryption.

(i)   Describe what is meant by the term encryption.

1 — Security risks and precautions

(ii)   State one reason why data encryption is required.

1 — Security risks and precautions

b)   State one other security method that may be used by an organisation to ensure a hacker cannot access data.

1 — Security risks and precautions

MARKS **STUDENT MARGIN**

2 Alex develops a program that will take in the radius of a circle, calculate the area and display the area of a circle. To help the user, the diagram on the right is also displayed.

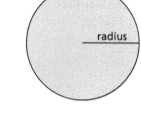

radius

a) The radius entered by the user is 57. Show how the value 57 would be stored as an 8-bit binary number.

| 1 | Data representation |

b) The text 'radius' is stored using extended ASCII.

Calculate the number of bits used to store the text 'radius'.

| 2 | Data representation |

c) The diagram is stored as a vector graphic.

(i) State the name of one of the objects used in the diagram.

| 1 | Data representation |

(ii) State two attributes of this object.

| 2 | Data representation |

d) The formula used to work out the area of a circle is area = πr^2 where π has the value 3.141592.

The value would be stored in a computer system using floating-point representation as:

$$0.3141592 \times 10^1$$

Identify the mantissa and exponent in the above floating-point representation.

| 2 | Data representation |

e) While the area program is being developed, it is executed using an interpreter. State one the purpose of an interpreter.

| 1 | Computer structure |

f) Name the parts of the computer system that will carry out the following tasks during the execution of the program.

(i) Carry the location of the radius variable in main memory.

(ii) Transfer the value of radius from main memory to the processor.

| 2 | Computer structure |

g) State the part of the processor that would calculate the area.

| 1 | Computer structure |

Database design and development

Longer questions with many parts, each part of a question being set within the same scenario. You need to apply your knowledge of designing databases or explain parts of a database design. You will also be asked to write and explain statements in SQL.

1 A credit union wishes to design and implement a database to store the information about customers and their purchases shown below. Each customer can use their credit union card for several purchases, provided they do not exceed their credit limit.

Customer	
Card Number	12359745
First name	Verena
Last name	Wayne
Town	Dumbarton
Start	01/12/2019
Expiry	01/12/2023
Credit Limit	£8 500.00
Current Balance	£175.87

Purchase	
TransactionID	35806
Card Number	12359745
Date of Purchase	03/09/2020
Amount	£78.52
Retailer	XYZ Sports

a) Complete the entity relationship diagram below by:
- drawing any missing the attributes from either entity
- drawing the relationship between the entities
- naming the relationship between the entities
- identifying any additional key fields.

| 5 | Design |

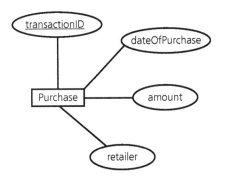

	MARKS	STUDENT MARGIN

b) State two implications of the General Data Protection Regulation (GDPR) for the credit union.

2 — Design

c) A data dictionary is also created at the design stage.

   (i) Name the attribute type that should be noted in the data dictionary for the start field.

1 — Design

   (ii) The retailer field has a presence check noted in the data dictionary. Describe the purpose of this validation.

1 — Design

   (iii) Other than a presence check, name and describe a suitable type of validation for the Current Balance field.

2 — Design

   (iv) Describe how the data dictionary is at the implementation stage.

1 — Design

d) The two tables are created.

Customer

cardNumber	firstName	lastName	town	start	expiry	creditLimit	currentBalance
12359745	Verena	Wayne	Dumbarton	01/12/2019	01/12/2023	8500.00	175.87
12365214	Pacorro	Bakhrushin	Glasgow	01/08/2019	01/08/2023	3200.00	1452.32
12365874	Georgena	Helstrom	Edinburgh	01/11/2019	01/11/2023	3200.00	445.65
12397741	Gene	Halmkin	Falkirk	01/07/2019	01/07/2023	1800.00	41.12
12459774	Tim	Lawlie	Aberdeen	01/10/2020	01/10/2024	3200.00	56.45
15975364	Kiley	Solomon	Aberdeen	01/09/2020	01/09/2024	4500.00	84.00
17874200	Luke	Bakhrushin	Glasgow	01/01/2019	01/01/2023	3400.00	31.36
20147963	Mala	Nevill	Edinburgh	01/11/2019	01/11/2023	5200.00	185.42
...							

Purchase

transactionID	cardNumber	dateOfPurchase	amount	retailer
35806	12359745	03/09/2020	78.52	ABC Sports
56022	12365214	02/08/2020	1000.00	Federers
37230	12365214	04/08/2020	80.00	NXShop
63348	12365214	05/08/2020	340.00	Stevenson
56102	12365214	03/08/2020	32.32	News & Bits
35482	12365874	03/10/2020	74.56	Holeys
41750	12397741	03/10/2020	521.74	Hippler
49172	12459774	16/09/2020	185.21	Petrol4U
20157	15975364	15/09/2020	179.32	J&G
35577	17874200	21/09/2020	275.41	JFD Holidays
35504	20147963	02/09/2020	74.56	DIY Galore
...				

(i) Design a query that could be used to create a list of all purchases made by Pacorro Bakhrushin. The list should show the date of the transaction, how much it was for, and the name of the retailer.

MARKS 4 — **STUDENT MARGIN** Design

Field(s)	
Table(s)	
Search criteria	
Sort order	

(ii) Design a query that could be used to create a list of card numbers issued after the start of 2020 and their expiry dates, with the ones about to run out soonest at the top of the list.

MARKS 4 — **STUDENT MARGIN** Design

Field(s)	
Table(s)	
Search criteria	
Sort order	

2 A database is created to store details of artists and their artwork in an exhibition. Each artist can exhibit one or more artworks.

The tables below show the artists and artworks currently ready for the exhibition.

Artist

artistRef	firstName	lastName
STU6UE9	Lindsay	Yadao
STU9N1A	Marg	Grasmick
STU9UNX	Ciara	Cobbley
STUF846	Edgar	Kanne
STUQVNJ	Corrinne	Jaret
STUTHTV	Tamesha	Veigel
STUW5BG	Laquita	Hisaw
STUWE7N	Evan	Zigomalas

Artwork

catalogRef	title	type	medium	price	artistRef
48-3002584	Sunrise	Painting	Acrylic	500	STU9UNX
42-4481371	Watty2	Painting	Acrylic	650	STUF846
28-5159690	Energy	Sculpture	Metal	250	STUWE7N
55-8546829	Crispy Duck	Print	Giclee	180	STUQVNJ
27-3244050	No Control	Drawing	Ink	300	STU6UE9
28-0104887	Whistles	Drawing	Ink	250	STU6UE9
52-6607930	Circles	Print	Linocut	175	STUQVNJ
10-3524425	Growth	Sculpture	Metal	3000	STUWE7N
41-5621622	Watty1	Painting	Acrylic	750	STUF846
82-9918190	Evening Sun	Painting	Oil	1000	STU9N1A
25-4443849	Lost	Painting	Oil	650	STU9N1A
84-1730998	Forest Light	Painting	Oil	2000	STUF846
07-9188670	Beachy Point	Painting	Oil	800	STUF846
96-5710434	Under the Sea	Sculpture	Plaster	700	STUW5BG
14-8648521	Sunset	Painting	Watercolour	350	STU9UNX
88-0525273	Phantom	Painting	Watercolour	1150	STUF846
87-5151318	Twins	Sculpture	Wood	1000	STUTHTV

		MARKS	STUDENT MARGIN

a) Describe the relationship that has been implemented between the two tables.

1 — Design

b) The following SQL statement is implemented in the database.

```
SELECT title, medium, price
FROM Artist, Artwork
WHERE Artist.artistRef = Artwork.artistRef AND firstName
= "Edgar"
AND lastName = "Kanne"
AND (medium = "Acrylic" OR medium = "Watercolour");
```

(i) Write the expected output from the SQL statement.

4 — Implementation

(ii) Describe how this expected output could be used to check that the SQL statement works correctly.

1 — Testing

c) Write an SQL statement to produce a list of artist names, artwork titles and prices of all the paintings or sculptures priced between £1000 and £1500.

5 — Implementation

d) Another artist called Sarafina Gunn is to be added to the artist table.
The SQL statement below is used to insert this record.

```
INSERT INTO Artist
VALUES ("STU4XAP", "Sarafina", "Gunn");
```

Explain why this record has to be added before any of her artworks can be added.

1 — Implementation

e) Sarafina has provided a wooden sculpture called Arrows priced at £950. It is given catalogue number 73-1234567.

Write an SQL statement to add this to the database.

2 — Implementation

f) The acrylic artworks by Edgar Kanne need to altered in the catalogue to show the medium as 'Acrylic on Canvas'.

The SQL statement below is used to make this change.

```
UPDATE Artwork
SET medium = "Acrylic on Canvas"
WHERE artistRef ="STUF846"
```

(i) Explain why the SQL statement will not produce the intended result.

1 — Testing

(ii) Rewrite the SQL statement to make it fit for purpose.

1 — Implementation

3 A shop keeps a database of Christmas stock items and suppliers. Parts of the tables are shown below.

Supplier		
supplierID	supplierName	town
1	Make it Sparkle	Katwell
2	House of Glitter	Frutchester
3	Twinkly Things Ltd	Sliyville
4	Festive Favours	Brouver
5	Special Gift Company	Aloville
6	Seasonal Gifts Ltd	Krury

Product					
supplierID	productCode	type	description	price	quantityStock
6	10618	Lights	Twinkle Garland	£9.99	124
3	43460	Gifts	Make Up Artistry Set	£19.99	42
6	44750	Gifts	Santa Card Holder	£7.99	89
3	44776	Gifts	Snowman Card Holder	£7.99	32
5	44890	Gifts	Clever Card Stand	£1.99	54
1	45110	Gifts	Star Card Holder	£8.99	589
3	45390	Cards	Bumper Pack of 50 Cards	£4.99	56
5	45420	Cards	Pack of Traditional Cards	£3.99	432
6	45560	Cards	Pack of Contemporary Cards	£3.99	223
2	44610	Gifts	Angel Card Holder	£9.99	78
4	45730	Gifts	Pack of 12 Cards with Pen	£3.99	76
4	46400	Wrapping	Giant Santa Sacks	£2.99	23
2	46850	Wrapping	Peel 'n' Stick Gift Tags	£1.99	250
4	48160	Decorations	Poinsettia Door Swag	£9.99	254
3	48470	Decorations	Santa Chair Covers	£4.99	345
6	48500	Decorations	Snowmen Chair Covers	£4.99	34
3	49450	Decorations	Deluxe Nativity	£9.99	213
...					

a) Based on the information shown above, show the expected output from this SQL statement.

```
SELECT productCode, price
FROM Product, Supplier
WHERE Product.supplierID = Supplier.supplierID
AND (supplierName = "House of Glitter" OR quantityStock
> 400)
ORDER BY price DESC;
```

b) Write an SQL statement that will produce a list of product descriptions and the supplier names of all cards with more than 100 in stock.

Web design and development

Longer questions with many parts, each part of a question being set within the same scenario. You need to apply your knowledge of designing webpages or explain parts of a website design. You will also be asked to write and explain statements in HTML and CSS.

1 The design for a webpage is shown below.

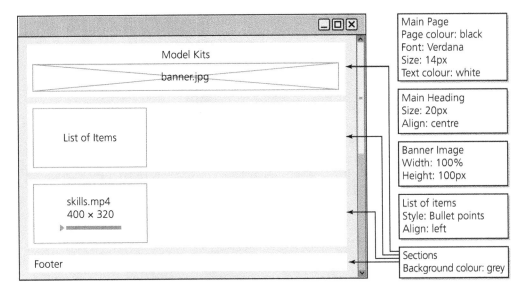

	MARKS	STUDENT MARGIN

a) Name this type of design.

1 — Design

b) The following CSS is used to style the main heading.

```
h1 {font-size:20px;
    text-align:center;}
```

Write a CSS statement to style the main page

5 — Implementation (CSS)

c) Name the HTML element that should be used to create the four sections on the page.

1 — Implementation (HTML)

d) The type of model kits to be included in the list of items are Aircraft, Cars, Dinosaurs and Spacecraft.

Write the HTML required to produce this list.

3 — Implementation (HTML)

e) A folder called images is created to keep the banner file and other pictures for the rest of the website. This folder is in the same directory as the model.html page.

Complete the HTML code below so the graphic is displayed.

```
<img src="_____" >
```

2 — Implementation (HTML)

f) The following code is used to display the video.

```
<video width="400" height="320" controls>
<source
src="skills.mp3"
type="video/mp4">
</video>
```

During testing, the video does not play. Describe the error in the code and how to correct it.

2 — Testing

g) The following code is included in the footer.

```
<p> Back to <a href="home.html"> home </a> page </p>
```

Show how this will appear when the page is viewed in the browser.

2 — Implementation (HTML)

		MARKS	STUDENT MARGIN

2 a) A music festival is planning to set up a new website to promote their next live event. Fans suggest that they would like to watch videos of bands and see photos from previous years when visiting the website.

State the functional requirements of the planned website necessary to meet the user requirements.

MARKS: 2 — **STUDENT MARGIN:** Analysis

Top Tip!

Make sure you can distinguish between what end users require of a website and what functions the website has to be capable of performing.

b) The organisers of the music festival decide to include a home page, with links to three different pages: Line Up, Venues and History. The user should also be able to return to the home page from each of these pages. The organisers also decide to include a link from the Line Up page to an outside ticketing agency website.

Draw the navigational structure for this website.

MARKS: 4 — **STUDENT MARGIN:** Design

Hint!

Start with the home page and draw boxes for each page mentioned. Use lines and arrows to show the direction of the links between pages.

c) The following HTML code is included on the Line Up page.

```
<title>Line Up</title>
```
Describe the purpose of the <title> element.

MARKS: 1 — **STUDENT MARGIN:** Implementation (HTML)

d) A collection of images, sound recordings and video clips from previous festivals are supplied by a number of different sources such as festival goers, media and press outlets, organisers and bands.

(i) Explain what the festival organisers must do to avoid prosecution under the Copyright, Designs and Patents Act when using these resources on the new website.

MARKS: 1 — **STUDENT MARGIN:** Design

(ii) Most of the photographs supplied are in the jpeg standard file format. State two reasons that this standard file format is suitable for use on webpages.

MARKS: 2 — **STUDENT MARGIN:** Design

(iii) The quality and file size of the photographs supplied vary widely. State two features of jpeg files which affect the quality of the images.

MARKS: 2 — **STUDENT MARGIN:** Design

(iv) State one standard file format used for sound recordings.

MARKS: 1 — **STUDENT MARGIN:** Design

(v) Describe the effect that altering the sample rate has on the quality of a sound file.

MARKS: 1 — **STUDENT MARGIN:** Design

e) The history page of the website contains a main heading and four headings for previous years.

The CSS rule below is used to style the main heading on the page.

MARKS STUDENT MARGIN

```
#pageheading {background-color: lightgreen;
              font-family: Verdana;
              font-size: 20px;
              color: black;
              text-align: center;}
```

(i) Write a single rule for all the year headings so they appear on the right side of the page and are formatted as white text on a pink background, using Georgia 14px.

5 | Implementation (CSS)

(ii) The web designers decide to use external CSS. Explain how this can help achieve consistency across multiple pages of the website.

2 | Implementation (CSS)

f) Name the type of addressing required in the link from the Line Up page to the ticketing agency website.

Implementation (HTML)

3 A webpage design is being implemented. Part of the unfinished page is shown below.

Section 1

Maths

Description of Maths topics in here

Computing

Description of Computing topics in here

Science

Description of Science topics in here

a) The developer needs to code a single CSS style for the three subject headings to ensure their formatting is consistent.

He knows he must use an id or class selector but is not sure which is required in this case. Name the correct type of selector that should be used here and give a reason for your choice.

2 | Implementation (CSS)

b) State the CSS declarations that should be used to change the position of the text to the centre and change the lettering to 14px.

2 | Implementation (CSS)

c) Part of the code for the page is shown below.

1 | Implementation (JavaScript)

```
<style>
body {background-color: lightgrey;}
</style>
…
<div onmouseover="this.style.backgroundColor='red'"
onMouseOut="this.style.backgroundColor='lightgrey'">
<p>Section 1</p>
<p>Maths</p>
<p>Description of Maths topics in here</p>
<p>Computing</p>
<p>Description of Maths topics in here</p>
<p>Science</p>
<p>Description of Maths topics in here</p>
</div>
```

When viewed in a browser the background of the section is either light grey or red.

Identify the JavaScript events used to implement this feature.

d) The developer wants to add this feature to the rest of the page so that each section will turn red in turn as it is highlighted. This extra code is added.

```
<div onmouseover="this.style.backgroundColor='red'">
<p>Section 2</p>
<p>English</p>
<p>English topics in here</p>
<p>French</p>
<p>French topics in here</p>
<p>Spanish</p>
<p>Spanish topics in here</p>
</div>
```

During testing, it is found that the effect is not what was required. Describe why the error occured and how it can be corrected.

e) Testing the JavaScript is one test that can be carried on a webpage. Name one other test that should be done on this webpage.

Section 1

Software design and development

Question number	Answer	Marks available
1	1 mark for describing that an earlier stage of the development process may need to be revisited as the result of something at a later stage, for example back to implementation after testing does not work as expected.	1
2	1 mark for inputs: length of cane 1, length of cane 2 1 mark for output: area of sail (or amount of paper needed)	2
3	1 mark for each input value (area, 5% extra option) with labelled instruction for user and data enter point 1 mark for each output value clearly labelled (Cost per m2, Total price) Turf Quote Area to turf [_____] m2 [✓] Add 5% extra to ensure coverage? Calculate Cost per m2 | Total £0.00 | £0.00	4
4	1 mark for data structure: array 1 mark for data type: string	2
5	1 mark for SeatType: string 1 mark for TicketPrice: real 1 mark for QuantityOrdered: integer	3
6	1 mark for text and concatenation included 1 mark for use of loop counter variable to give 1,2,3,4,5 1 mark for use of array and loop counter variable to display fruit names Example in SQA reference language: `SEND ("Fruit" & index & " is called " & fruits[index]) TO DISPLAY`	3
7	1 mark for function: Random 1 mark for one parameter of Random function: 0,1,2,3,4 or 5 or activityList	2
8	1 mark for values less than 0, e.g. −20 1 mark for values more than 100, e.g. 200	2
9	1 mark for any parcelweight between 1 and 20, e.g. 10 1 mark for any parcellength between 1 and 40, e.g. 20	2
10	1 mark for identifying that logic errors produce the incorrect output. 1 mark for describing that in the list there are three people 18 and over eligible to vote but program output is 2.	2

Question number		Answer	Marks available
11	a)	1 mark for digits are not unique as each number generated independently of others and not checked to see if it is the same as a previous one (random numbers could be 1,2,4,3,1 which are not unique digits). **or** Five-digit code is not produced at all, as five random numbers are added together in Line 13 (largest possible value for code variable is 9 + 9 + 9 + 9 + 9 which is 45 only has two digits).	1
	b)	1 mark for use of loop to repeat Lines 8–12 **or** 1 mark for use of array to store values generated to avoid use of five variables **or** 1 mark for use of concatenation inside a loop to build up code as each digit generated instead of Line 13	1
			25

Computer systems

Question number		Answer	Marks available
1		1 mark for 173	1

128	64	32	16	8	4	2	1
1	0	1	0	1	1	0	1

gives 128 + 32 + 8 + 4 + 1 = 173

| 2 | | 1 mark for 00110100 | 1 |

128	64	32	16	8	4	2	1
0	0	1	1	0	1	0	0

gives 32 + 16 + 4 = 52

Question number		Answer	Marks available
3		1 mark for mantissa: 2342849 1 mark for exponent: 5	2
4		1 mark for 56 bits (1 character = 8 bits so 7 characters = 7 × 8 = 56)	1
5		1 mark for ALU (Arithmetic Logic Unit)	1
6		1 mark for unique address for each location	1
7		1 mark for any one of: ▶ settings on monitors ▶ power down settings ▶ leaving computers on standby	1
8		1 mark for install firewall	1
9		1 mark for description of encoded data is not readable if intercepted so private data not accessible unless you have encryption key.	1
			10

Database design and development

Question number		Answer	Marks available
1		1 mark for the end-user requirements cannot be met as the database does not provide the functionality needed. 1 mark for extra fields – department and paygrade – need to be included to provide the functional requirements.	2
2		Any two from: ▶ data processed lawfully ▶ data used for declared purpose only ▶ data stored limited to that needed for declared purpose ▶ data must be accurate ▶ data must not be kept longer than necessary ▶ data must be held securely	2
3	a)	1 mark for each key in Pupil Entity ▶ Primary key is pupilID ▶ Foreign key is group 1 mark for primary key in Class Entity ▶ Primary key is group	3
	b)	Many Pupils have 1 Class **or** 1 Class has Many Pupils	1
4		1 mark for each A: Primary Key B: restricted choice: Purchasing, Production, Sales, Despatch C: Number	3
5		1 mark for each search criteria ▶ city = "Glasgow" ▶ year formed < 1910 1 mark for sort order ▶ average ticket price Ascending	3
6		1 mark for each sort with department sort done first ▶ `department DESC` ▶ `lastName ASC`	2
			16

Web design and development

Question number		Answer	Marks available
1		1 mark for analysis	1
2		1 mark for company name top and centre 1 mark for logo below name 1 mark for introduction text full width of page 1 mark for bullet list with three correct items **Trndi** Logo Introduction text in here • Designers • Products • Materials	4

3		1 mark for correct <head> and </head>
		1 mark for correct <p> and </p>
		1 mark for correct <a and </a>
		
		`<html>`
		`<head>`
		`<title> Creating a Website </title>`
		`</head>`
		`<body>`
		`<h1>Website heading</h1>`
		`<p>The first section of text goes in here</p>`
		`<a href="http://w3schools.com"> Click here for help with HTML</a>`
		`</body>`
		`</html>`
			3

4		1 mark for using number items 1 mark for correct items listed one below each other 1 Contents 2 Introduction 3 Revision 4 Test	2
5		1 mark for absolute	1
6		1 mark for correct use of <img src = > 1 mark for correct path and filename "pix/rome.jpg" `<img src="pix/rome.jpg">`	2
7		1 mark for class selector	1
8		1 mark for id is unique on a page – there is only one heading. 1 mark for class is used to name many elements the same, so they can be formatted in the same way.	2
9		1 mark for (Not fit for purpose) as nothing on webpage about dates of upcoming debates as specified in requirements.	1
			17

Section 2

Software design and development

Question number			Answer	Marks available
1	a)		1 mark for Inputs: ▶ the number of steps taken each day (31 integers greater or equal to 0) 1 mark for Process: ▶ add up the 31 numbers ▶ check if the total is greater than or equal to 1 000 000 1 mark for Output: ▶ appropriate message about reaching the target 1 000 000 or not	3
	b)		1 mark for structure diagram	1
	c)		1 mark for one correct use of assignment: ▶ set total to 0 (0 is assigned to total variable) ▶ add number of steps for day to total (new total is assigned to total variable) ▶ get number of steps for the day (number of steps entered is assigned to a variable)	1
	d)		1 mark for repeat 31 times	1
	e)	(i)	1 mark for input validation	1
		(ii)	1 mark for running total within a loop	1
2	a)		1 mark for pseudocode	1
	b)		1 mark for conditional loop	1
	c)		1 mark for calculation 1 mark for assigning result to same variable Example in SQA reference language: `SET number TO number + 2`	2
	d)		1 mark not fit for purpose as does not give expected output 1 mark for explanation as it does not display the odd numbers less than 6 – the output is 3,5,7	2
3	a)		1 mark for flowchart	1
	b)		1 mark for the actions to hook a duck and read the number on it are repeated three times	1
	c)	(i)	1, 1, 1 or 2, 2, 2 or 3, 3, 3 or 4, 4, 4 etc. – all three numbers the same	2
		(ii)	1, 2, 3 (= 6) or 1, 5, 3 (= 8) etc. – all three numbers added make a total less than 10	
	d)		1 mark for 1, 2, 2 will be awarded second prize as total 1 + 2 + 2 is less than 10 1 mark for 1, 2, 2 will also be awarded third prize as two numbers are the same	2
	e)	(i)	1 mark for each of three comparisons (1&2, 2&3 and 1&3) 1 mark for using OR Example in SQA reference language: `IF duck1=duck2 OR duck1=duck3 OR duck2=duck3 THEN`	4
		(ii)	1 mark for threeSame	1

Question number			Answer	Marks available
		(iii)	1 mark for name of technique	2
			1 mark for description of use in this code	
			► Internal commentary could be used to explain each line is doing – Line 13 checks if all the numbers are the same.	
			or	
			► White space – could be used to break the code into sections – space between Line 15 and Line 16 to separate off first and second prize sections.	
4	a)		1 mark for data structure: array	2
			1 mark for data type: character or string	
	b)		1 mark for function: Length (find length of array)	2
			1 mark for parameter: votes/name of array	
	c)		1 mark for fixed loop	1
	d)		1 mark correct use of IF/ELSE statement	4
			1 mark to correct use of array element in comparison	
			1 mark for correct comparison to text value	
			1 mark for adding 1 to total	
			Example in SQA reference language:	

			`IF votesList[index] = "A" THEN`
			`    SET totalA TO totalA + 1`
			`ELSE IF votesList[index] = "B" THEN`
			`    SET totalB TO totalB + 1`
			`ELSE`
			`    SET totalC TO totalC + 1`
			`END IF`	

5	a)		1 mark for identifying that rate will store an amount of money – a numeric value with a decimal part	1
	b)		1 mark for calculation of normal pay (hours * rate)	4
			1 mark for calculation of overtime pay (overtime * (rate * 1.5))	
			1 mark for calculation of weekend work (rate * 2 * weekend)	
			1 mark for total calculation being assigned to weeklyPay variable	
			Example in SQA reference language:	
			`SET weeklyPay TO (hours * rate) + (overtime * (rate * 1.5)) +` `    (rate * 2 * weekend)`	
	c)		1 mark for correct use of array and index	3
			1 mark for assigning calculation to total variable	
			1 mark for adding to total	
			Example in SQA reference language:	
			`SET total TO total + julyPay[number]`	
				44

Computer systems

Question number			Answer	Marks available
1	a)	(i)	1 mark for data is encoded/scrambled	1
		(ii)	1 mark for to make data unreadable if intercepted during transmission	1
	b)		1 mark for install a firewall	1
2	a)		1 mark for 00111001	1
	b)		1 mark for 48 bits 1 mark for radius has six letters and ASCII uses 8 bits per character so $6 \times 8 = 48$ bits	2
	c)	(i)	1 mark for line or ellipse	1
		(ii)	1 mark for line attribute: x coordinate, y coordinate or line colour 1 mark for ellipse attribute: fill colour, x coordinate, y coordinate or line colour	2
	d)		1 mark for mantissa: 3141592 1 mark for exponent: 1	2
	e)		1 mark for interpreter is used to translate high-level language to machine code	1
	f)	(i)	1 mark for address bus	1
		(ii)	1 mark for data bus	1
	g)		1 mark for Arithmetic Logic Unit (ALU)	1
				15

Database design and development

Question number		Answer	Marks available
1	a)	1 mark for adding creditLimit and currentBalance attributes to Customer entity 1 mark for adding cardNumber attribute to Purchase entity 1 mark for 1 (Customer) to Many (Purchase) relationship drawn 1 mark for relationship named appropriately such as makes 1 mark for identifying cardNumber in Purchase entity as foreign key 	5

Question number			Answer	Marks available
1	b)		Any two from: ▶ data must be processed lawfully by the credit union ▶ credit union must declare the purpose for which the data will be used (used for declared purpose only) ▶ credit union must collect only the data required for the declared purpose ▶ credit union must ensure data is accurate ▶ delete personal data if members leave the credit union (not keep data longer than necessary) ▶ store data securely ▶ data can't be shared without customer permission ▶ must show customer their stored details when requested Answers must refer to credit union club implications and not customer implications.	2
	c)	(i)	1 mark for date	1
		(ii)	1 mark for presence check ensures that the field is not left empty – a value must be entered for the retailer.	1
		(iii)	1 mark for name of validation: range check 1 mark for description: currentBalance should be greater than 0 and less than or equal to the CreditLimit.	2
		(iv)	1 mark for the plan outlined in the data dictionary is used as a guide/reference to actually set up fields and their characteristics.	1
	d)	(i)	1 mark for correct fields 1 mark for both tables 1 mark for firstname criteria 1 mark for lastName criteria Alternatively, search criteria cardNumber=12365214 would be acceptable. As this is design, equi-join not required and use of logical operator (AND) is not essential.	4

Field(s)	dateOfPurchase, retailer, amount
Table(s)	Customer, Purchase
Search criteria	firstName="Pacorro" AND lastName="Bakhrushin"
Sort order	

Question number			Answer	Marks available
		(ii)	1 mark for each row of the grid	4

Field(s)	cardNumber, expiry
Table(s)	Customer
Search criteria	start >= 1/1/2020
Sort order	expiry ascending

Question number			Answer	Marks available
2	a)		ONE Artist exhibits MANY Artworks	1
	b)	(i)	1 mark for correct fields with no extras 1 mark for each correct record identified	4

title	medium	price
Watty2	Acrylic	650
Watty1	Acrylic	750
Phantom	Watercolour	1150

Question number			Answer	Marks available
2	b)	(ii)	1 mark for the expected output would be compared to the actual output when the query is executed to ensure the results match.	1

	c)		1 mark for each line
			
			`SELECT title, price, firstName, lastName`
			
			`FROM Artist, Artwork`
			
			`WHERE Artist.artistRef = Artwork.artistRef`
			
			`AND (type = "Painting" OR type = "Sculpture")`
			
			`AND (price >=1000 and price <=1500);`
				5

	d)		1 mark for referential integrity (The artworks are created by artists so their details must be in the database first before they can be linked to the artwork table where the artistRef is the foreign key.)	1

	e)		1 mark for each line
			
			`INSERT INTO Artwork`
			
			`VALUES ("73-1234567", "Arrows", "Sculpture", "Wood", 950, "STU4XAP");`
				2

	f)	(i)	1 mark for this statement will change all artworks by artist STUF846 to be Acrylic on Canvas and not just the two Acrylic artworks.	1

		(ii)	1 mark for WHERE clause (as other clause is exactly the same as given in question)
			
			`(UPDATE Artwork`
			
			`SET medium = "Acrylic on Canvas")`
			
			`WHERE artistRef="STUF846" and medium="Acrylic";`
				1

3	a)		1 mark for only two columns (product code and price) 1 mark for each of four correct records 1 mark for correct sort order of product codes <table><tr><td>productCode</td><td>price</td></tr><tr><td>44610</td><td>£9.99</td></tr><tr><td>45110</td><td>£8.99</td></tr><tr><td>45420</td><td>£3.99</td></tr><tr><td>46850</td><td>£1.99</td></tr></table>	6

	b)		1 mark for each line
			
			`SELECT description, supplierName`
			
			`FROM Supplier, Product`
			
			`WHERE Supplier.supplierID = Product.supplierID`
			
			`AND type="Cards"`
			
			`AND quantityStock>100;`
				5

				47

Web design and development

Question number			Answer	Marks available
1	a)		1 mark for wireframe	1

	b)		1 mark for styling body selector created with correct structure: – name – brackets – semi-colon to separate declarations
			1 mark for each declaration: background-color, font-family, font-size,color
			Example:
			`body  {background-color: black;`
			        `font-family: Verdana;`
			        `font-size: 14px;`
			        `color: white;}`
				5

	c)		1 mark for div	1

	d)		1 mark for correct use of \<ul> and \</ul> tags
			1 mark for correct use of \<li> and \</li> tags
			1 mark for correct list items – Aircraft, Cars, Dinosaurs and Spacecraft
			`<ul>`
			`<li>Aircraft</li>`
			`<li>Cars</li>`
			`<li>Dinosaurs</li>`
			`<li>Spacecraft</li>`
			`</ul>`
				3

	e)		1 mark for path 1 mark for filename and extension: images/banner.jpg	2
	f)		1 mark for identifying error with file type used 1 mark for changing .mp3 to .mp4 in Line 3	2
	g)		1 mark for correct text displayed 'Back to home page' 1 mark for correctly identifying anchor as home: Back to <u>home</u> page	2
2	a)		1 mark for each The system must be able to: ▶ play video ▶ display graphics	2

Question number			Answer	Marks available
2	b)		1 mark for LineUp, Venues and History pages 1 mark for double headed arrows to/from home page 1 mark for tickets page 1 mark for single arrowhead from LineUp page to tickets 	4
	c)		1 mark for any one of: ▶ defines a title in the browser toolbar ▶ provides a title for the page when it is added to favourites ▶ displays a title for the page in search-engine results	1
	d)	(i)	1 mark for seek permission from/pay all the copyright holders to use their photos/sound recordings/video clips on the website.	1
		(ii)	Any two from: ▶ high colour depth gives good quality image ▶ small file size as jpg is compressed format ▶ downloads quickly due to small file size ▶ format is compatible with all browsers	2
		(iii)	Any two from: ▶ resolution ▶ colour depth ▶ compression rate	2
		(iv)	1 mark for mp3 or wav	1
		(v)	1 mark for increase in sampling rate increases quality	1

	e)	(i)	1 mark for class created with correct structure: dot – name – brackets – semi-colon to separate declarations
			1 mark for each declaration: background-color, font-family, font-size, color, text-alignment
			Example:
			
			`.year{background-color: pink;`
			`        font-family: Georgia;`
			`        font-size: 14px;`
			`        color: white;`
			`        text-align: right;}`
				5

Question number			Answer	Marks available
	e)	(ii)	1 mark for CSS rules stored in a single document and linked to each webpage. 1 mark for all pages have same formatting applied or changes to formatting done in one place so all pages updated to keep consistent.	2
	f)		1 mark for absolute addressing	1
3	a)		1 mark for class selector 1 mark for reason – class used to format multiple elements on the same page (id is unique on a page so no good for three headings)	2
	b)		1 mark for text-align: center 1 mark for font-size: 14px	2
	c)		1 mark for onmouseover/onmouseout	1
	d)		1 mark for Section 2 changes to red when mouse over but does not change back to light grey when cursor moved away. 1 mark for add onmouseout into Section 2 div element: `onMouseOut="this.style.backgroundColor='lightgrey'"`	2
	e)		1 mark for any one of: ▸ check the page matches the design ▸ check the formatting is applied correctly (Note: no links so not an acceptable test in this scenario)	1
				46

Practice paper 1

Section 1

Total marks: 25

Attempt ALL questions.

There is no strict allocation of time for each section. However, each paper should be completed in 2 hours as this is the length of time for the SQA National 5 papers.

MARKS

1 Convert the decimal number 87 into 8-bit binary.

1

2 FairBrock Medical practice wants a website to provide information to patients. They specify that the home page must include the following:
- an introduction to the practice
- a section about team members
- the practice logo
- a link to the appointments page
- a link to the prescriptions page
- a link to the test results page

The design below is created to show the proposed home page.

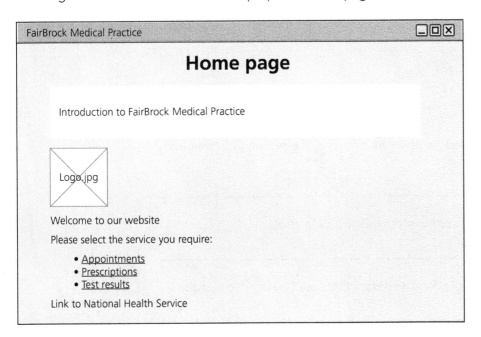

MARKS

a) State the design technique used.

1

_____

b) Evaluate the proposed webpage design in terms of its fitness for purpose.

1

_____

_____

c) The medical practice is advised to use a firewall and encryption to keep data secure.

(i) Explain the purpose of a firewall.

1

_____

(ii) Explain how encryption can keep data secure.

1

_____

3 A quiz program is being written. To answer the question, the user must enter the letter (A, B, C or D)

Question: What is the capital of Poland?
A   Kraków
B   Warsaw
C   Łódź
D   Wrocław
Enter your answer (A, B, C or D): B

To make sure that only A, B, C or D is accepted, the following algorithm is designed.

Algorithm

1. Get answer from keyboard
2. While answer is not A or B or C or D
3.   Display error message
4.   Get answer from keyboard
5. End loop

The letter B is an example of a normal test data value that could be used to test the program.

a) State a standard code used to represent this type of test data in a computer system.

1

_____

b) State the number of bits used to store this test data value.

1

_____

c) State one example of exceptional test data that could be used to test the program.

1

_____

4 The output below was produced by running a query in a database.

City				
name	admin	population	areaSqKm	popDensity
London	ENG	8 992 166	1295.0	6945
Manchester	ENG	557 344	98.5	5661
Bristol	ENG	576 813	112.0	5129
Birmingham	ENG	1 159 114	230.0	5044
Newcastle	ENG	285 491	57.9	4931
Liverpool	ENG	583 132	123.0	4729
Sheffield	ENG	549 362	122.0	4485
Belfast	NIR	336 610	91.5	3678
Bangor	NIR	63 090	19.6	3225
Glasglow	SCO	623 260	146.0	4284
Edinburgh	SCO	498 050	119.0	4203
Aberdeen	SCO	198 000	58.5	3383
Dundee	SCO	148 600	46.3	3209
Paisley	SCO	77 310	26.6	2901
Dunfermline	SCO	54 050	19.2	2811
Cumbernauld	SCO	50 430	21.5	2343
Livingston	SCO	57 030	27.1	2101
Cardiff	WAL	351 884	71.4	4930
Swansea	WAL	185 166	49.1	3773

Complete the SQL statement used to produce this sorted output.   **2**

```
SELECT name, admin, population, areaSqKm, popDensity
FROM City
ORDER BY _____
```

5 A travel agency requires a program for currency conversion. The user will enter the name of the currency they have and the name of the currency they want to buy. They will then enter the amount to be converted. The program will then use the appropriate exchange rate to do the conversion and the user will be informed how much of the second currency they can buy.

Using the information above, design a user interface for the program.   **3**

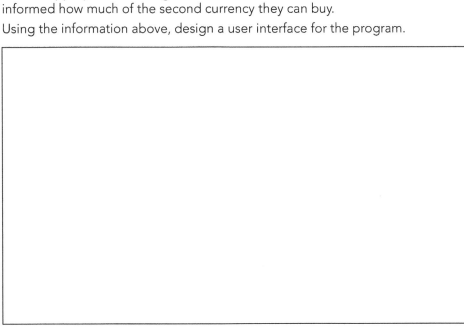

6

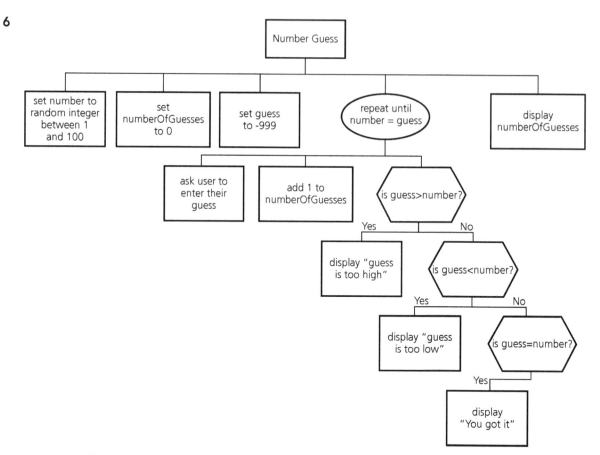

a) State the type of loop shown in the design above.

1

_____

b) The design is tested. The random number is 80. For the following inputs, state the outputs.

3

Inputs	Outputs
90	
78	
80	

7 Design the navigation structure for the following website.

2

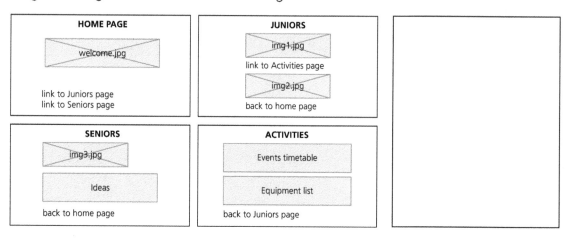

8 A database table 'Result' is shown below. It stores information about times taken in the 100 metres at a sports competition. To qualify for the next competition, runners need to run 12.37 seconds or better.

Result		
CompetitorNumber	school	timeTaken
103	Lowtown	11.84
298	Rivermouth	12.37
349	Hillside	12.69
427	Gilbert	12.31
526	Central	12.64

Complete the SQL statement below to remove the competitors who did not qualify.

```
DELETE FROM Result

WHERE _____
```

1

9 The HTML code below is used to create a webpage.

```
<html>
<head>
<style>
div {text-align: left;}
h1 {text-align: center;}
</style>
<title> Resort Facts</title>
</head>
<body>
<h1>Nevis Range</h1>
<div>
A mountain resort located at Fort William in the heart of
the Scottish Highlands
<ul>
<li>12 ski lifts</li>
<li>20 km trails</li>
<li>highest elevation 1221m</li>
</ul>
</div>
</body>
</html>
```

Draw how this webpage will look when viewed in a browser.

Some of the content has already been added.

2

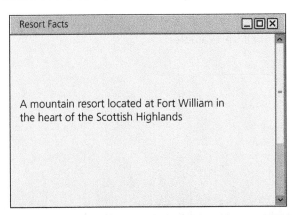

10 A database stores information about birds and the photographs taken in someone's garden.

Bird		
birdCode	type	conservationStatus
B1	Robin	Green
B2	Greenfinch	Green
B3	Goldfinch	Green
B4	BlueTit	Green
B5	Woodpecker	Green
B6	Blackbird	Green
B7	Starling	Red
B10	Bullfinch	Amber
B11	Chaffinch	Green
B12	Yellowhammer	Red

Photo				
photoID	birdCode	date	time	location
DSC003	B1	03/05/2020	12:10	Fence
DSC004	B5	03/05/2020	14:15	Tree
DSC005	B3	03/05/2020	17:22	Feeder
DSC006	B5	03/05/2020	18:46	Feeder
DSC007	B12	04/05/2020	13:12	Ground
DSC008	B2	04/05/2020	14:20	Feeder
DSC009	B5	04/05/2020	14:27	Fence

Read the SQL statement below.

```
SELECT type, date, location
FROM Bird, Photo
WHERE Bird.birdCode = Photo.birdCode
AND (conservationStatus= "Red" OR location= "Tree");
```

a) Complete the table below to show the expected output from this SQL statement.

type	date	location

2

b) State the part of the processor where the SQL conditions will be evaluated.

1

_____

Section 2

Total marks: 85

Attempt ALL questions

11 A program is required to calculate and display the cost of fuel for a journey. The user enters the fuel type, the price for a litre of fuel, the number of miles for the journey and the mileage per gallon (mpg) for the vehicle.

A possible user interface for the program is shown below.

1

1. Enter the fuel details
Select fuel type — Unleaded
Enter price per litre — 108.38 pence
2. Enter the mileage for the journey to the nearest mile
50 miles
3. Enter vehicle miles per gallon (must be between 20 mpg and 80 mpg)
40 mpg
Total cost of fuel

Gallons of fuel required (mileage/mpg)	1.25	gallons
Litres of Fuel required (gallons * 4.546)	5.68	litres
Cost of fuel (litres * price)	615.5984	pence
Total Cost of fuel	**£6.16**	

a) Describe two processes that will be carried out by the program.

2

_____

_____

b) State the data types that will be required to store the values of the following inputs.

2

type of fuel	
price per litre in pence	

c) The program uses input validation to ensure the miles per gallon (mpg) entered is between 20 and 80.

```
...
Line 15      RECEIVE mpg FROM (INTEGER) KEYBOARD
...
```

Using a programming language of your choice write the code to validate the mpg, ensuring that only acceptable values can be entered and a suitable error message is displayed for incorrect values.

3

d) The program works out the cost of the fuel in pence.

...

Line 25   SET cost TO litres * price

...

(i) Using a programming language of your choice, write the code to convert the cost to pounds and display this to two decimal places, along with the words shown on the user interface.

3

(ii) The cost of fuel 615.5984 would be stored in a computer system using floating-point representation as:

0.6155984×10^3

Identify the mantissa and exponent in the above floating-point representation.

2

12 Linzi is creating a website called GardenWeb about birds that visit her garden. Linzi designed the home page and then coded it.

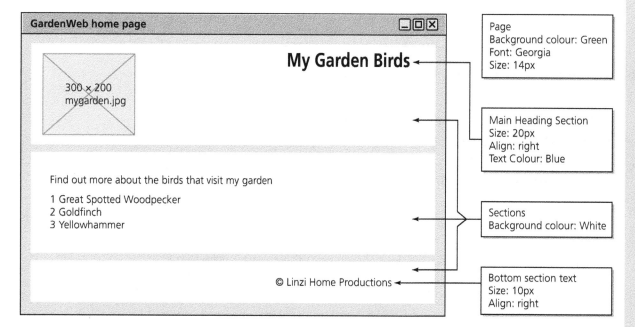

HTML	CSS

`<html>`
`<head>`
`<title>GardenWeb home page</title>`
`<link rel="stylesheet"`
`href="styles.css">`
`</head>`
`<body>`
`<div>`
`<h1>My Garden Birds</h1>`
`<img src="mygarden.jpg">`
`</div>`
`<div>`
`<h2> May 2020</h2>`
`Find out more about the birds that visit my garden`
`<ul>`
`<li> Great Spotted Woodpecker</li>`
`<li> Goldfinch</li>`
`<li> Yellowhammer</li>`
`</ul>`
`</div>`
`</body>`
`</html>`
	`body   {background-`
	`        color:Green;`
	`        font-family:Georgia;`
	`        font-size:14px;}`
	`div    {background-`
	`        color:White;}`
	`h1     {text-align:center;`
	`        font-size:20px;`
	`        color:Blue;}`
	`img    {width:600px;`
	`        height:200px;}`
	`#foot  {text-align:right;`
	`        font-size:10px;}`

a) While implementing the design, Linzi missed out the bottom section. Identify three other differences between the sketched design and the finished page.

_____

_____

_____

3

b) Write the HTML code for the bottom section.

3

c) When testing the page, the image does not appear. Describe a problem that may have caused this to happen.

1

_____

Linzi has placed her own photographs, video and sound recordings into a folder called media. The structure of the website is shown below.

1

📁 > GardenWeb	📁 > GardenWeb > media
📁 media	📄 garden.jpg
🌐 goldfinch.html	📄 goldfinch.jpg
🌐 home.html	🔺 woodpecker.mp3
📄 styles.css	🔺 woodpecker.mp4
🌐 woodpecker.html	📄 woody1.jpg
🌐 yellowhammer.html	📄 woody2.jpg
	📄 yellowhammer.jpg

2

d) Each bird page must include a link back to the home page.
Complete this HTML code to link the goldfinch page back to the home page.

2

```
< _____ href=" _____ ">Back

to Home Page<_____ >
```

e) The photographs are bit-mapped graphics.

(i) Describe how a bit-mapped graphic is represented in the memory of a computer system.

2

_____

_____

(ii) State two reasons the standard file format used above is suitable for photographs on webpages.

2

_____

_____

MARKS

f) The following onmouseover and onmouseout events are coded on the woodpecker page.

```
<img src="media/woody1.jpg"
onmouseover="this.src='media/woody2.jpg'"
onmouseout="this.src='media/woody1.jpg'" >
```

(i) Name the language used to code these events.

_____

1

(ii) Describe the effect of the two events when viewing the page.

_____

_____

2

g) Complete the following HTML code included on the woodpecker page.

```
<audio src="_____"
controls="controls"></audio>
```

2

1

h) Explain why Linzi does not need to consider the Copyright Design and Patents Act when creating her website.

_____

13 An event company runs workshops in Science, Technology, Engineering and Mathematics topics. The organisers currently hold information in paper records. Some examples are shown below.

TutorID **Tut243**
Forename **Joe**
Surname **King**

Subject
☐ Science
☒ Computing
☐ Engineering
☐ Design technology
☐ Maths

Workshop **w101**
TutorID **Tut243**
Topic **Relational databases**

Level ☐ Beginners   ☒ National 5
      ☐ Higher   ☐ Adv Higher

Workshop **w205**
TutorID **Tut243**
Topic **Web design**

Level ☐ Beginners   ☐ National 5
      ☒ Higher   ☐ Adv Higher

Each tutor can run up to five workshops. Each workshop has only one tutor and is always run by a specialist in the subject. The organisers often need to find information such as who is running a certain workshop, which workshops are available for a specific subject or level and which tutors can teach each subject.

The organisers decide the information would be more useful in a database so they could quickly find information.

a) Use the information above to identify two functional requirements.

2

_____

_____

b) Use the information provided to complete the entity relationship diagram below by:
- drawing any missing attributes
- drawing the relationship between the entities
- naming the relationship between the entities
- identifying any additional key attributes.

4

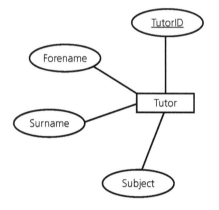

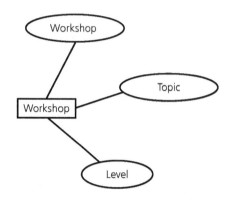

A data dictionary is designed for the new database. Part of it is shown below.

Entity Name: Tutor					
Attribute Name	Key	Type	Size	Required	Validation
TutorID	PK	A	B	yes	length=6
Forename		text	20	yes	
Surname		text	20	yes	
Subject		text	17	yes	C

c) State the missing information to complete A, B and C in the data dictionary.

3

_____

_____

d) Before storing the information, the organisers need to consider the implications of GDPR legislation. Explain why this is necessary.

1

_____

_____

14 The design of a program is shown below.

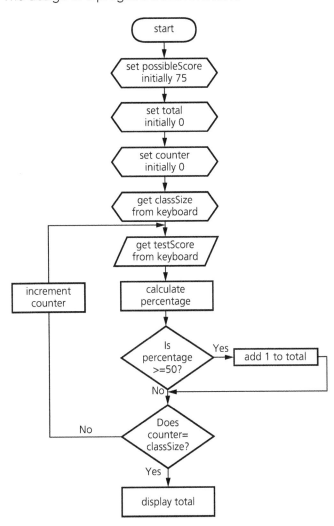

a) State the design technique that has been used.

1

_____

b) Several programming constructs will be required to implement the program.
  (i) State one example from the design where an assignment construct is
      required.

1

_____

  (ii) State the condition in the selection construct.

1

_____

  (iii) Identify the standard algorithm used in the design.

1

_____

c) The program is implemented using a fixed loop.

...

```
Line 5    DECLARE possibleScore INITIALLY 75
Line 6    DECLARE total INITIALLY 0
Line 7    DECLARE classSize INITIALLY 15

...

Line 10   _____

Line 11       RECEIVE testScore FROM KEYBOARD
Line 12       SET percentage TO testScore/possibleScore*100
Line 13       IF percentage >= 50 THEN
Line 14           SET total TO total +1
Line 15       END IF
Line 16   END FOR

...

Line 28   SEND  "The number of passes equals" & total
          TO DISPLAY
```

(i) Using a programming language of your choice write the code in Line 10 to start the fixed loop.

2

(ii) Identify the operator used to concatenate the program above.

1

d) Testing is carried using the following test data:
10, 15, 20, 25, 30, 35, 40, 45, 50, 55, 60, 65, 70, 75, 80

(i) State the output produced for this test data.

1

(ii) Name the type of error that exists in the program.

1

(iii) Describe how the error could be corrected.

1

15 A relational database is used to store details of players in an ice hockey league. Some of the data is shown below.

Club		
clubname	town	region
Jets	Jedburgh	Borders
Snappers	Inverness	Highland
Demons	Kirkcaldy	Fife
Rascals	Rosyth	Fife
Drafters	Kirkcaldy	Fife
Eddys	Edinburgh	Lothian

Player					
playerID	forename	surname	position	age	clubname
P101	Rory	Deir	Right Wing	14	Eddys
P102	Sam	Croza	Left Wing	15	Demons
P103	Arif	Aziz	Defenceman	14	Rascals
P104	Jean	Gagnon	Defenceman	16	Drafters
P105	Jacques	Tremblay	GoalTender	19	Snappers
P106	Niki	Ivanov	Left Wing	16	Jets
P107	Kev	Kyle	Right Wing	14	Drafters
...	...	...	...	...	...

a) Design a query that would output the names of all the Defencemen that play for clubs in Kirkcaldy.

4

Fields	
Tables	
Search Criteria	

b) The administrators of the league want to view the names of all the players in Fife who are eligible for the Under 15 regional team. Player must be 15 or under to qualify.

```
SELECT playerID, position, age
FROM Player, Club
WHERE Player.clubname = Club.clubname
AND age = 15
AND town = "Fife"
```

Although the query runs, it is not fit for purpose as it does not produce the expected output.

State two reasons why the above statement does not give the expected output.

2

_____

_____

c) Another SQL statement is implemented to show all the Eddys players. The output is shown below.

surname	age
Maguire	19
Smith	18
Blok	17
Jaconelli	17
Armstrong	16
Hernandez	16
Able	15
Booker	15
Crighton	15
Deir	14
Donald	14

Write the SQL statement that produces this output.

d) A fan of the ice hockey league can buy a season ticket to watch all the games of their favourite club. A program is being developed to allow season tickets to be purchased. Here is a possible user interface for this part of the program.

Season Ticket Purchase			
Name:			
Year of birth:			
Ticket options (select one only):	☐ 1. Standard £50 (50% off under 18s)	☐ 2. Premier £75 (50% off under 18s)	☐ 3. Ultimate £100 (25% off under 18s)
	Click here to calculate		

State the number of inputs required by this part of the program.

_____

e) The program design shows how the ticket cost is calculated:

Algorithm

1. Initialise adult prices

2. Get inputs

3. Assign ticket category

4. Work out current age

5. Calculate discount rate for under 18s

6. Calculate ticket price

7. Display ticket price

Refinement

1.1 Set standardPrice to 50

1.2 Set premierPrice to 75

1.3 Set ultimatePrice to 100

1.4 Set discount to 0%

3.1 if option1 is selected then ticketcategory is "S"

3.2 if option2 is selected then ticketcategory is "P"

3.3 if option3 is selected then ticketcategory is "U"

4.1 currentAge is CurrentYear take away yearOfBirth

Using a design technique of your choice, refine Step 5.

16 A new band called MacRokk want to create a website and specify the following content.
- The MacRokk logo
- An introduction to the band
- A page with band member photos and biographies
- A page with tour dates and video clip of the band playing on stage
- A page with details of their latest album and sample audio clips of tracks

a) The band logo is created using vector graphics.

(i) State the object used to create the lightning bolt shape.

_____

(ii) The fill colour attribute of this object is stored as grey. State one other attribute that is stored.

_____

b) Two versions of the logo are created – logo.gif and logo.jpg
The following CSS is used to format the page background.

```
body{background-color:lightgrey}
```

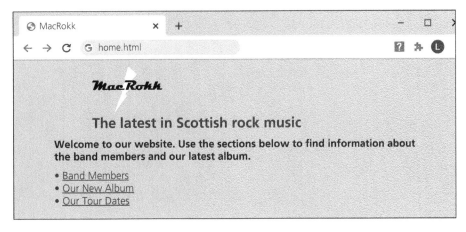

(i) Complete the HTML code below so the graphic is displayed.

```
<img src="_____ " >
```

(ii) Explain your answer.

1

_____

c) The tour dates are shown on the webpage below.

Tour Dates

Ayr
Date: 14/6/2022
Venue: Ayr Town Hall

Edinburgh
Date: 19/6/2022
Venue: Assembly Rooms

Inverness
Date: 22/6/2022
Venue: IronWorks

Aberdeen
Date: 27/6/2022
Venue: Beach Ballroom

To achieve consistency, the same style is applied to every page of the website. Describe how this is done using external CSS.

2

_____

_____

d) The text 'Tour Dates' is styled using the following rule:

```
#mainhead  {text-align:center;
           font-family:Verdana;
           font-size:20px;
           color:slategray;}
```

(i) State the type of selector used in the above style.

1

_____

(ii) Each gig location has white text in 18 pixels. Write a single style rule that could be used to style all of the gig locations.

3

17 A game is being played by five people. The program below awards the winner 1 point.

...

```
Line 10      DECLARE allScores INITIALLY [0,0,0,0,0]
Line 20      DECLARE playerName INITIALLY ["Anna", "Baz",
             "Colum", "Dev", "Ellena"]
Line 30      RECEIVE winnerName FROM KEYBOARD
Line 40      FOR index FROM 0 TO 4 DO
Line 50          IF winnerName = playerName[index] THEN
Line 60              SET winnerPosition TO index
Line 70          END IF
Line 80      END FOR
Line 90      SET allScores[winnerPosition] TO
             allScores[winnerPosition]+1

...

Line 200     SEND allScores[0] TO DISPLAY
Line 210     SEND allScores[1] TO DISPLAY
Line 220     SEND allScores[2] TO DISPLAY
Line 230     SEND allScores[3] TO DISPLAY
Line 240     SEND allScores[4] TO DISPLAY
```

...

a) Name the data structure used in Line 10 and state the data type that it is used to store.

Name of data structure: _____

Data type stored: _____

2

b) (i) State the input entered at Line 30 if the following output is produced.

0
0
1
0
0

Input: _____

1

(ii) The code used to produce the output is inefficient. Using a programming language of your choice, rewrite the code in Lines 200 to 240 in a more efficient way.

3

(iii) State the variable that should be used to display the name of the player beside their score to make the output more understandable to the user.

_____

1

c) Identify a technique used by this programmer to make the code readable.

_____

1

Practice Paper 2

Section 1

Total marks: 25

Attempt ALL questions.

There is no strict allocation of time for each section. However, each paper should be completed in 2 hours as this is the length of time for the SQA National 5 papers.

1 Convert the following 8-bit binary number into denary.
   1101 1001

   1

2 Identify the type of validation suitable for a database field called season which has four values – spring, summer, autumn and winter.

   1

3 Line 1   RECEIVE length FROM KEYBOARD
   Line 2   SET result TO length ^ length
   Line 3   SEND result TO DISPLAY

   a) State the output from the code above if the user enters the value 3.

   1

   b) State the processor component that calculates the result.

   1

4 The following HTML code is styled using the CSS shown below.

HTML	CSS
`<body>`	`body`
`<h1>Cities in Scotland</h1>`	`{background-color:Blue;`
`<p>Edinburgh</p>`	`font-family:Georgia;`
`</body>`	`font-size:14px;}`
	`h1`
	`{text-align:center;`
	`font-size:20px;`
	`color:white;}`

   State the size of the text "Edinburgh"

   1

5 Bartek writes a program using a high-level language.

During testing, the following error report appears.

| Line 3: error: ';' expected |
| Line 6: error: <identifier> expected |
| Line 9: error: BOOL is undefined |
| Line 13: error: For without Next |
| 4 errors |

a) Name the type of translator that has been used.   1

_____

b) Identify the type of error found at Line 3.   1

_____

6 A database stores information about planets.

Planets

name	diameterKm	meanTempC	moons	ringSystem
Mercury	4879	167	0	No
Venus	12104	464	0	No
Earth	12756	15	1	No
Moon	3475	−20	0	No
Mars	6792	−65	2	No
Jupiter	142984	−110	79	Yes
Saturn	120536	−140	82	Yes
Uranus	51118	−195	27	Yes
Neptune	49528	−200	14	Yes
Pluto	2370	−225	5	No

a) State the attribute type most suitable for the meanTempC field.   1

_____

The following query is designed.

Field(s)	name, moons
Table(s)	Planets
Sort Order	moons descending, name ascending
Search Criteria	meanTempC is > −30

b) Complete the table showing the expected output from this query.   2

name	moons

MARKS

7 In Scotland, you can vote in an election if you are 18 or over. A program is written to count the number of people in a list eligible to vote.

```
Line 1        DECLARE total INITIALLY 0
Line 2        DECLARE ages INITIALLY [12,34,32,16,18,19,20]
Line 3        FOR loop FROM 0 TO 6 DO
Line 4            IF ages[loop] > 18 THEN
Line 5                SET total TO total +1
Line 6            END IF
Line 7        END FOR
Line 8        SEND total TO DISPLAY
```

Evaluate the fitness for purpose of the program. Give a reason for your evaluation.

2

8 The code below is used to create a webpage.

```
<html>
<head>
<style>
body {background-color: Red;}
h1 {color: white; text-align: center;}
img {width: 200px; height: 200px;}
</style>
</head>
<body>
<h1>London</h1>
<img src="arch.jpg">
<p>On our website, you will find helpful facts and tips for
planning your trip to London</p>
<ul>
<li><a href="stay.html"> Accommodation</a></li>
<li><a href="eat.html"> Eating out</a></li>
<li><a href="visit.html"> Tourist Attractions</a></li>
<li><a href="transport.html"> Getting around</a></li>
</ul>
</body>
</html>
```

Describe two tests that should be carried out on this page.

2

9 The following program is incomplete.

```
Line 10      RECEIVE number1 FROM KEYBOARD
Line 11      RECEIVE number2 FROM KEYBOARD
Line 12      SET answer TO number1/number2
Line 13      <display result of calculation>
```

Normal Test data	
number1	10
number2	5
Expected Output	The answer is 2

a) Using a programming language of your choice, write the line of code required at Line 13 to produce the expected output, with the words and answer, as shown in the test table.

2

b) During testing, the following test data values are used.

Exceptional Test data	
number1	10
number2	0
Expected Output	Error

Name the type of error that occurs with this test data.

1

10 A school stores pupil data in a database. It must not keep data longer than necessary. State one other implication for the school in relation to personal data.

1

11
```
Line 10    IF timeTaken >90 THEN
Line 11        SET lives TO lives - 1
Line 12    END IF
```

Name the part of the computer system that:

a) temporarily stores the value of lives.

1

b) carries the location where the variable lives is stored in main memory.

1

c) transfers the value of the variable lives from main memory to the processor.

1

MARKS

12 Council tax is a charge paid by households to the local authority. Householders are sent a bill based on the property value. Households can select 10 monthly payments or 12 monthly payments.

A single person household is entitled to 25% discount.

The design below is used to work out the monthly payment.

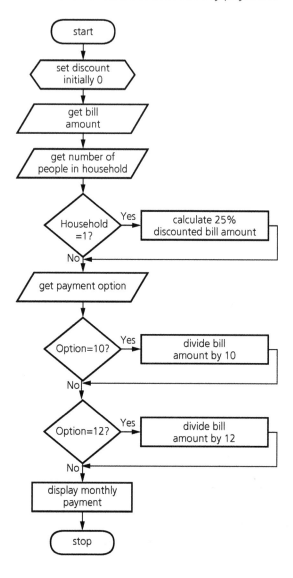

a) Name the design technique used above.

1

_____

b) Identify a conditional statement used in the design.

1

_____

c) Test the design by stating the expected output for the following:

(i) a single person with a bill of £1200 who opts for 10 monthly payments

1

_____

(ii) a large household with a bill of £2400 that selects 12 monthly payments

1

_____

Section 2

Total marks: 85
Attempt ALL questions.

13 Craig makes replacement registration plates for cars. The cost for each character on a registration plate is £2.50 and the cost of including a badge is £5.
Customers can order one front plate, one back plate or both.

Craig wants to create an app to work out the cost of the new plates.
Algorithm

1. Initialise values
2. Get customer requirements
3. Calculate cost of order
4. Display total cost

Refinement

1.1 Set characterPrice to 2.50
1.2 Set badgePrice to 0.00

2.1 Get registration without spaces (max seven characters)
2.2 Get quantity of plates required (1 or 2)
2.3 Get badge requirement (True or False)

3.1 Find number of characters in registration
3.2 If badge requirement is True then update badgePrice to 5
3.3 Calculate cost of plates

a) Identify the design technique used above.   1

_____

b) State the programming construct required at Step 1.1.   1

_____

c) State the data types that will be required to store the values of the following inputs:

   (i) Registration   1

_____

   (ii) Badge requirement   1

_____

d) State the standard algorithm required in Step 2.2 to ensure only 1 or 2 is entered.

_____

e) Identify the predefined function and its parameter(s) that will be used in Step 3.1.

_____

_____

f) Using a design technique of your choice, refine Step 3.3.

g) Gaz has the registration XYZ123. He wants two plates – one front and one back – with the Scotland badge on both. State the expected output from the proposed program.

_____

14 Karen and her work colleagues enter teams into a charity triathlon which involves running, swimming and cycling a total distance of 50 km.

Details are stored for each team member and their training activities in preparation for the event. Here is part of the database.

TeamMember

employeeID	team	employeeName	age	teamCaptain
101	1	Alison	55	✓
102	2	Jaxon	34	✓
103	1	Zuleika	19	
104	1	Sam	42	
105	3	Rohaan	27	✓
106	2	Piotr	32	
107	2	Lian	25	
108	3	Kacia	33	

Activity

activityID	type	activityDate	timeTaken	distanceKm	employeeID
1	Run	01/04/2020	40.20	5	101
2	Swim	02/04/2020	28.43	1	101
3	Cycle	03/04/2020	24.32	10	101
4	Run	01/04/2020	62.27	10	102
5	Run	04/04/2020	38.25	5	101
8	Swim	06/04/2020	55.46	2	102

a) State the type of validation that should be used to ensure the following:

(i) the distanceKm field only accepts values between 1 and 50

1

_____

(ii) the timeTaken field is not left empty

1

_____

b) Design a query to find the names and times of all the people aged over 40 who have completed a 10 km run. The times taken should be listed with the fastest first.

5

Field(s)	
Table(s)	
Search Criteria	
Sort Order	

c) The following SQL statement is used to add information about Alexandra to the TeamMember table.

```
INSERT INTO TeamMember
VALUES (109, 3, "Alexandra", 22, False);
```

(i) State the attribute type used for the teamCaptain field.

1

_____

(ii) Write the SQL statement to add Sam's 20 km cycle to the database using activityID 6. She completed it on 5/4/2020 in 44.27 minutes.

2

_____

_____

(iii) State why the details about Sam should be added to the database before details about her training activities.

1

_____

15 Fizical Fitness require a website to promote their new business and ask a web design company to create the website with pages for exercise tips, workout videos and activity plans.

a) During the analysis stage, the web design company ask Fizical Fitness staff about who is going to be using their website and what these users should be able to do when using the website.

Explain why it is important to clarify the end-user requirements before designing a website.

2

_____

_____

b) During the design process, the web designers create a low-fidelity prototype. Explain the purpose of a low-fidelity prototype.

1

_____

c) The website design includes some stick characters doing physical activities.

(i) These images are stored as vector graphics. Describe how vector graphics are stored in a computer.

_____

_____

2

(ii) Some of the characters are animated. State a suitable file format for storing these images.

_____

1

d) The design also includes a sound recording of motivational tips on exercising.

The audio software being used to make the recording offers two settings for sampling rate shown below.

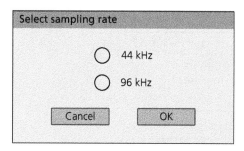

Select sampling rate

○ 44 kHz

○ 96 kHz

Cancel   OK

(i) In order to have the best sound quality, state which sampling rate should be selected for recording.

_____

1

(ii) State the effect of recording the sound at the best quality on the size of the sound file.

_____

1

The website is created and part of the file structure is shown below.

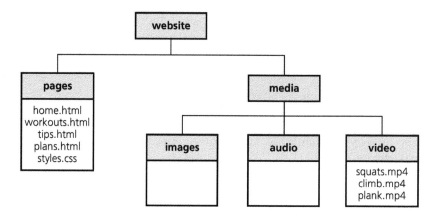

website

pages
home.html
workouts.html
tips.html
plans.html
styles.css

media

images

audio

video
squats.mp4
climb.mp4
plank.mp4

e) **(i)** State the type of addressing that should be used to link the workout.html page back to the home.html page.

_____

(ii) Complete the code from the workout.html page to display the squats video.

```
<video controls>
<source src="_____" type="video/mp4">
</video>
```

(iii) The video clips are stored using a compressed file format. State one benefit to the end-user of using a compressed format for these files.

_____

f) Part of the 'Tips' page is shown below. All the text is written using <p> elements.

> Physical Activities
>
> Cardio Activity
>
> Cardio is good for burning calories and will help make you more physically fit. It improves your heart and lung function.
>
> Strength Activity
>
> Strength activities help make your muscles stronger and boost your metabolism.

The subheadings 'Cardio Activity' and 'Strength Activity' are styled as follows:

```
.subheading{text-align:left;
          font-size:14px;
          background-color:yellow;
          color:black;}
```

The main heading 'Physical Activities' should be larger than the subheadings, in yellow lettering and in the middle of the page.
Write a single style rule that could be used to style only this heading.

16 A new retail park in Malaga, Spain, wants to offer shoppers the opportunity to pay for parking using an app on their mobile phone.

The shopper will be asked to enter the parking bay number, their car registration and the length of stay required. The program will work out and display the amount to be charged.

a) Using the information above, identify any inputs and outputs for the program.

_____

_____

b) The parking charges are displayed on the board at the car park.

P		
Tariff	Duration	Cost per minute
A	For each minute from 1 to 30	0.021584 €
B	For each following minute	0.034175 €
Maximum stay 4 hours		

State the data type that will be required to store the following values in the program.

(i) Cost per minute for tariff A

_____

(ii) Number of minutes to stay

_____

(iii) The value of 0.021584 would be stored in a computer system using 'floating-point representation' as:

$$0{\cdot}21584 \times 10^{-1}$$

Identify the mantissa and exponent in the above floating-point representation.

Mantissa _____

Exponent _____

c) The program makes sure that only acceptable values can be entered for the number of minutes.
Using a programming language of your choice, complete Line 18.

```
...
Line 13    REPEAT
Line 14        RECEIVE minutes FROM <the touchscreen
               keyboard>
Line 15        IF <minutes is not valid> THEN
Line 16            SEND "Maximum stay is 4 hours" TO DISPLAY
Line 17        END IF
Line 18    _____
...
```

d) Another part of the program is shown below.

```
...
Line 34   SET costA TO 0.021584
Line 35   SET costB TO 0.034175
Line 36   IF minutes<=30 THEN
Line 37       SET parkingcharge TO minutes*costA
Line 38   ELSE
Line 39   _____
Line 40   END IF
Line 41   <display parkingcharge to 2 decimal places>
...
```

(i) Using a programming language of your choice, write the code in Line 39 to calculate the total parking charges for the number of minutes entered.

4

(ii) State the predefined function and a parameter that could be used in Line 41.

2

Predefined Function: _____

Parameter: _____

e) When testing the program the following output summary is given on the app.

Date	4 May
Car registration	SM16BDF
Parking Bay	134
Parking Charges for 120 minutes	3.72€
Exit Time	12.06

Other than working out the cost of parking, state one other process that the program has carried out.

1

_____

17 A city farm creates a website to provide information to visitors about the animals and attractions. The code below is for one of the webpages.

HTML	CSS
| ```html
<html>
<head>
<title> City Farm </title>
<link rel="stylesheet"
  href="styles.css">
</head>
<body>

<div class ="section"> Down on
  the Farm </div>

<div id = "activities">

<p>Here are the latest arrivals
  </p>
<img src="piglets.jpg">

<p>Things to do</p>
<p> Visit the stables </p>
<p> Feed the chickens</p>
<p> Take a tractor ride</p>

</div>
<p class="section"> <a
  href="home.html">Back to Home
  Page</a> </p>
</body>
</html>
``` | ```css
img    {width: 300px;
        height: 200px;}
div    {font-size: 20px;
        color: White;}


.section
   {background-color: DarkBlue;
    text-align: center;}


#activities
   {background-color: Red;}
``` |

a) Describe the formatting applied to the 'Down on the Farm' text.

_____

_____

2

b) The code uses both class and ID selectors. Explain the difference between these selectors.

_____

_____

_____

2

c) The code `<p>Here are the latest arrivals </p>` is edited to include the onmouseover event shown below.

```
<p onmouseover="this.style.color='blue'" >Here are
the latest arrivals </p>
```

(i) Name the programming language used to add this event.

1

_____

(ii) Explain how the page creator should test this event works correctly

2

_____

_____

_____

d) Identify the file format used for the image on this webpage.

1

_____

e) Rewrite the code for the three 'Things to do' as a bullet list of items.

2

f) The navigation link 'Back to Home Page' is tested. The links returns the user to the home page correctly but after being clicked, the text turns blue and is no longer visible on the background.

Write a CSS rule to change the colour of the anchor to yellow.

2

g) Describe one technique used to evaluate whether a webpage is fit for purpose.

1

_____

_____

18 A vehicle repair workshop wants to store information about repairs carried out on vehicles so that they can search for details of jobs carried out and find customer contact details quickly.
The entity relationship diagram for the system is shown below.

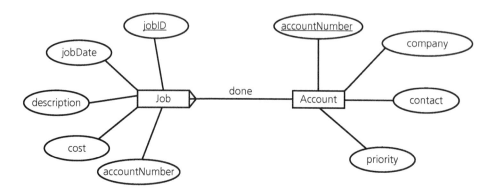

a) Write the correct attribute names in the appropriate boxes below to show the primary and foreign keys used in the database.

Entity	Primary Key	Foreign Key
Job		
Account		

2

b) State the cardinality of the relationship shown in the diagram.

1

c) The database is implemented and data entered into the tables.

The SQL command INSERT is used to add a new account but following error is produced.

> **!** The accountNumber field must contain seven digits

Explain why this error has occurred.

2

d) Some of the data in the database is shown below.

Account			
accountNumber	company	contact	priority
1134566	Framework UK	Fraser	True
1365320	Baynes	Craig	True
2087502	GHJ	James	True
4355326	CJ Kelly	Russell	False
4587901	Quinn Ltd	Gordon	False

Job				
jobID	jobDate	description	cost	accountNumber
10132	14/06/2020	Repair Clutch	250	1134566
10133	14/06/2020	MOT	55	1134566
10134	14/06/2020	Service	240	1365320
10135	15/06/2020	Brake Fluid	45	2087502
10136	15/06/2020	Service	240	4355326
10137	20/06/2020	Wiper Blade	12	2087502

The following SQL statement is implemented in the database.

```
SELECT jobDate, company
FROM Account, Job
WHERE  Account.accountNumber = Job.accountNumber
AND description = "Service";
```

(i) Describe the end-user requirements that necessitated this query.

2

_____

_____

(ii) Write an SQL statement to find a list of jobs done for companies with priority status which cost less than £100. The list should display the jobID, company name and contact person.

5

e) CJ Kelly have been upgraded to priority status. The following SQL statement is written to carry out the change.

```
UPDATE Account
SET priority = True
WHERE priority = False;
```

(i) Explain why the SQL statement will not produce the intended result.

1

_____

(ii) Rewrite the incorrect SQL line to correct the error.

1

f) Describe how the vehicle repair company can evaluate their database.

1

_____

g) At the end of each working day, the vehicle repair workshop switch off their computer systems to reduce energy use.
Describe two other methods of reducing energy use of a computer system.

2

_____

_____

Practice Paper 1

Section 1

Question			Answer	Marks available	Commentary, hints and tips
1			01010111	1	$87 = 64 + 16 + 4 + 2 + 1$ | 128	64	32	16	8	4	2	1
---	---	---	---	---	---	---	---
0	1	0	1	0	1	1	1	 Make sure your answer has eight bits by adding leading zeros.
2	a)		wireframe	1	A wireframe indicates the intended layout of the page and shows the position of all text elements on the page, any media elements (images, audio clips and video clips) and the position of all hyperlinks on the page.
	b)		Website is not fit for purpose. 1 mark for any one of: ▶ missing section about team members ▶ extra external link to NHS	1	To evaluate a website to see if it is fit for purpose, it is necessary to review what the requirements were for the website. In this question, carefully work through the bullet points in the question and check if they have all been met. Then work through the sketch and check for anything extra that has been added.
	c)	(i)	To restrict access to a network.	1	This is necessary for the medical practice to try to prevent hacking as the information in their computer systems will be sensitive, personal information.
		(ii)	data is coded/unreadable	1	If sensitive data, such as medical test results, is encrypted before transmission then even if it is intercepted it will not be readable without the encryption key, hence keeping the data more secure.
3	a)		extended ASCII	1	The data type for the single letter B is character or string. Extended ASCII is an 8-bit code used to store characters. Other answers might be ASCII or Unicode but they are beyond the scope of the National 5 course.
	b)		8 bits	1	The test data value is one character so only eight bits used to store it. (ASCII – 7 bits, Unicode – 16bits)
	c)		1 mark for any one of: ▶ a single letter such as G except A, B, C or D ▶ any symbol or numeric value such as 1 or $ ▶ a string such as 'Warsaw'	1	Exceptional test data refers to value which are not valid. Step 2 of the algorithm tells us the valid answers so any other character would be exceptional.

Question			Answer	Marks available	Commentary, hints and tips
4			`admin ASC, popDensity DESC`	2	At National 5, it is common to get questions about sorting in two fields. The first sort is usually easy enough to spot – here the admin column is in alphabetical or ascending order (ASC). To see the next sort, look at the data that has the same value in the first sorted field – that means just look at the English cities (ENG) or just look at the Scottish cities (SCO). Look for a column that has data in order for those sections only. In this question, it is the popDensity column that is listed from highest to lowest (DESC). Also note that this question is about writing code so make sure you spell the field names accurately as given in the table otherwise you will not be awarded the marks.
5			1 mark for each ▸ entry of currency1 and currency2 with labelled input area ▸ entry of amount to exchange with labelled input area ▸ output area displaying converted amount in new currency	3	You need to sketch a suitable interface for the program – as long as it shows a) where the inputs are to be entered with a suitable instruction for the user and b) the result of the conversion with a suitable output area. Hint Text interface Graphical interface

Question			Answer	Marks available	Commentary, hints and tips
6	a)		conditional loop	1	In a structure diagram, a loop is shown in an oval symbol with the actions to be repeated listed below it. The symbol contains the number of times to repeat if it is a fixed loop or it contains the conditions for the repeating to continue or end if it is a conditional loop. In this question, the oval symbols contains the words 'repeat until number = guess'. This is a condition for when the repeating has to end so the design shows a conditional loop.
	b)		1 mark for each set of output statements 	Inputs	Outputs
---	---
90	Guess is too high
78	Guess is too low
80	You got it NumberOfGuesses=3		3	Outputs are shown as display actions in the structure diagram. Don't forget to include the action after the loop has finished.
7			1 mark for each ▶ juniors and seniors page linked to the home page with double headed arrows ▶ activities page linked to juniors page with double headed arrow	2	Start with drawing a box for the home page and then read the home page sketch and look for 'links'. Draw boxes for pages that are linked to the home page and connect them with single arrow from the home page. Then look at the sketches for these new boxes/pages and again look for links. Draw boxes for links to new pages and arrows to indicate whether the link is to the new page or back to previous page.
8			timeTaken > 12.37	1	Make sure you understand the scenario given in the question – the fastest runners qualify – so 12.37 seconds or better means you need to delete records where the time taken is more than that. Also note that this question is about writing code so make sure you spell any field names accurately as given in the table otherwise you will not be awarded marks.

Question			Answer	Marks available	Commentary, hints and tips
9			1 mark for each ▶ big heading 'Nevis Range' centre aligned ▶ left aligned, bullet point list with the three correct items, in correct order	2	Read the HTML body to identify the page content and the tags used for layout. Read the CSS style declarations in the head to see how to format the content. "Nevis Range" are the first words to appear on the page. <h1> indicates heading of size 1. The style declaration h1 {text-align: center;} will position this text in the middle of the page. <div> is used to contain the sentence already done for you and three unordered (<ul>) list items (<li>). The style declaration div {text-align: left;} positions the list at the left of the page. **Resort Facts** ☐☐☒ **Nevis Range** ① A mountain resort located at Fort William in the heart of the Scottish Highlands • 12 ski lifts • 20 km trails ② • highest elevation 122 m
10	a)		1 mark for each row | type	date	location
---	---	---
woodpecker	3/5/2020	Tree
yellowhammer	4/5/2020	Ground		2	You may find it useful to highlight records that match the criteria given to help you work out the answer for this one. Two birds have 'red' status (birdCode B7 and B12) One bird has 'tree' location (birdCode B5) The search is done across both tables, so you are looking for photos of birds that match one or other of the criteria. There are no photos of B7, so only the photo of bird B12 with photoID DSC007 matches the first search criteria. There are three photos of B5 but only DSC004 matches the second search criteria.
	b)		ALU	1	The Arithmetic and Logic Unit performs all the arithmetic operations such as +, −, *, / and logical operations such as AND, OR, NOT.
				25	

Section 2

Question			Answer	Marks available	Commentary, hints and tips
11	a)		Any two from: ▸ calculate gallons of fuel required (mileage divided by mpg) ▸ calculate litres of fuel required (gallons * 4.546) ▸ calculate cost of fuel (litres * price) ▸ convert cost of fuel from pence to pounds	2	To identify processes you have to look for things that the program does with the data entered – it could be a calculation, a search, a function being applied, a value being validated.
	b)		1 mark for each ▸ type of fuel: string ▸ price per litre: real	2	The example given for type of fuel is Unleaded, which contains letters. This will need to be stored as a string data type. The example given for price per litre is 108.38 which is a number with a decimal part. This will need to be stored as a real number. Although the programming language you have used may refer to a real data type as SINGLE, DOUBLE or FLOAT, in the exam you should use real.

	c)		1 mark for each
			
			▸ conditional loop used
			▸ correct loop condition for valid data
			▸ error message
				3	This is the standard algorithm for input validation and should be written with a conditional loop – could be Repeat or While loop.
					
					You should write your answer in the programming language used during your course, e.g. Python, Java, VB, LiveCode.
					
					Hint
					
					In SQA reference language using Repeat…Until:
					
					`REPEAT`
					
					`RECEIVE mpg FROM KEYBOARD`
					
					`IF mpg < 20 OR mpg > 80 THEN`
					
					`    SEND "Error, please enter again" TO DISPLAY`
					
					`END IF`
					
					`UNTIL mpg >= 20 AND mpg <= 80`
					
					In SQA reference language using While:
					
					`RECEIVE mpg FROM KEYBOARD`
					
					`WHILE mpg < 20 OR mpg > 80 DO`
					
					`SEND "Error, please enter again" TO DISPLAY`
					
					`RECEIVE mpg FROM KEYBOARD`
					
					`END WHILE`

Question			Answer	Marks available	Commentary, hints and tips

	d)	(i)	1 mark for each
			▶ divide cost by 100 to get pounds
			▶ round to 2 decimal places
			▶ concatenate message and cost message
				3	You should write your answer in the programming language used during your course e.g. Python Java, VB, LiveCode.
					This can be written in either 1, 2 or 3 instructions.
					Hint
					In SQA reference language:
					`SET cost TO cost/100`
					`SET totalcost TO round(cost,2)`
					`SEND "Total cost of fuel is £"`
					`   & totalcost TO DISPLAY`

		(ii)	mantissa:6155984 exponent:3	2	The mantissa is the part of a number located after a decimal point and the exponent is used to show where the point should be placed.
12	a)		Any three from: ▶ alignment for h1 should be right not centre ▶ width for img should be 300px and not 600px ▶ <h2> May 2020 </h2> not included in the design ▶ <ul> list used but design shows ordered list	3	There is a lot of reading and cross checking required in this one. Highlighting things as you go will be useful to help check things off. The style descriptions point to where they are to be applied on the webpage, so compare them with the CSS code. The sketch shows the content so compare this with the HTML content.

	b)		1 mark for each
			▶ creating section using <div> and </div>
			▶ use correct id
			▶ adding correct text content
				3	You are asked to write code for a section – other sections in this code are marked by using <div>.
					The CSS rule for the bottom section uses the #foot selector so this tells you that you must include an id and name it foot.
					Look at the sketch to find the content for the section.
					`<div id="foot">`
					`© Linz Home Productions`
					`</div>`

	c)		1 mark for any of: ▶ wrong file name used ▶ wrong path given/image is in a different folder ▶ wrong file type used ▶ image does not exist	1	Testing that media displays properly is one of the normal webpage tests. You have probably experienced this same problem during your course – think about how you fixed it.

Question		Answer	Marks available	Commentary, hints and tips
d)		1 mark for each ▸ correct anchor tags <a> and </a> ▸ correct file name and extension home.html	2	Links are created using an anchor element with <a> at the start and </a> at the end with the text that will be clicked to activate the link in the middle. The text is given in this question – 'Back to Home Page'. The href attribute is used to indicate the destination of the link, so look for the file to be taken to in the diagram and check out its location. If it is in the same folder as the goldfinch page then you don't need to include a path, just the file name and its extension. `<a href="home.html">Back to Home Page</a>`
e)	(i)	1 mark for each ▸ graphic is composed of pixels ▸ each pixel stored as a binary value	2	This example of a black and white graphic shows how a bit mapped image is made of pixels. A white pixel is stored as a 0 and a black pixel is stored as a 1. If more colours are used then each pixel is represented by a group of bits instead of just one.
	(ii)	Any two from: ▸ high colour depth gives good quality image ▸ small file size as jpg is compressed format ▸ downloads quickly due to small file size ▸ format is compatible with all browsers	2	Look at the media folder – you can see a variety of file types held there. You should recognise jpg as a standard file format for photographs.
f)	(i)	JavaScript	1	JavaScript is the scripting language that can be used to create and manipulate HTML elements.
	(ii)	1 mark for each ▸ image called woody1 is displayed when page is loaded but when user moves cursor over this image it changes to another image called woody2 ▸ when user moves cursor away from the woody2 image it reverts back to original image called woody1	2	A JavaScript event is programmed to happen to an HTML element – so your answer should refer to both the event that occurs and the element that it effects.

Question			Answer	Marks available	Commentary, hints and tips
	g)		1 mark for correct path: media/ 1 mark for audio file name: woodpecker.mp3	2	The start of the code indicates that it is an audio clip and the instruction indicates that this code appears on the woodpecker page. You should recognise mp3 as a standard file format for audio. There is only one mp3 file in the media folder so use the correct filename and file extension. You also need to note the location in relation to the woodpecker page location to get the correct path. `<audio src="media/woodpecker.mp3" controls ="controls" ></audio>`
	h)		Linzi took the photos herself so she owns the copyright.	1	Text and media are subject to copyright legislation and the relevant permission must be sought before they can be published. In this scenario, the files belong to Linzi so she does not need to seek permission or pay fees to use them on her website.
13	a)		Any two from: ▶ search workshops for tutor details. ▶ search workshops for certain levels. ▶ search workshops for certain subjects.	2	Functional requirements describe the processes and activities that the system has to perform to meet the end-user needs. Read the question carefully, highlighting any search, sort, insert, delete or update tasks that the user wants to be able to do. It is easy to lose marks here by just restating the end-user needs – when writing your answer, ensure you are clear about what the system has to do to meet these needs.
	b)		1 mark for each ▶ missing attribute added: only tutorID attribute added to Workshop entity ▶ one (Tutor) to many (Workshop) relationship drawn ▶ relationship named appropriately such as runs, takes, teaches ▶ identify PK Workshop in Workshop entity and FK TutorID in Workshop entity	4	Work through the bullet points in the question so you don't miss out anything here. Missing attributes – watch out for attributes like Subject – it is only one attribute with a list of choices. If you include extra attributes, you will not be awarded the mark even if you do include the correct missing attribute. Naming the relationship – try to pick a verb that describes what ONE of the entities does with the other. Avoid 'has' if you can. Drawing relationships – you need to identify a 1:M relationship between the entities. Ask two questions: always start with ONE.

Question			Answer	Marks available	Commentary, hints and tips
					From left to right ask ONE tutor TEACHES how many workshops? Answer: MANY.
					(So, the relationship in that direction is 1:M – leave the one side as it is and add a 'crowsfoot' on the 'many' side.)
					From right to left ask ONE workshop IS TAUGHT BY how many tutors? Answer: ONE.
					(So, the relationship in that direction is 1:1 – no need to add any more to the diagram as both answers here are 1.)
	c)		1 mark for each A: text B: 6 C: restricted choice – limited to the five subjects listed	3	The example given for a TutorID is Tut243 which contains letters and numbers. The attribute type needs to be text. The example given for a TutorID is Tut243 which has six characters. You might think it could be longer but the validation given in the data dictionary shows a length check so the maximum number of characters is six. The attribute size is 6. The example given for a subject is Computing but it is one of a list of choices. The validation needs to be restricted choice. Make sure you refer to the scenario – either list the subjects or refer to the five subjects in your answer.
	d)		Data stored is personal data and so the organisers need to adhere to the GDPR regulations.	1	The General Data Protection Regulation is a law relating to personal data protection and privacy.
14	a)		flowchart	1	A flowchart shows the order of execution of instructions from the start at the top to the end at the bottom.

Question			Answer	Marks available	Commentary, hints and tips
	b)	(i)	1 mark for any of: ▶ set possible score to 75 ▶ set total to 0 ▶ set counter to 0 ▶ add 1 to total ▶ store classSize value entered at keyboard ▶ store testScore value entered at the keyboard ▶ store percentage calculated	1	Assignment is the programming construct used to put a value into a variable. Assignment can be used to: ▶ declare an initial value ▶ store a value entered at the keyboard in a variable ▶ store the result of calculation ▶ update a value already held in a variable.
		(ii)	1 mark for any of: ▶ percentage>=50? ▶ counter=classSize?	1	A selection construct is used to follow one path or another based on a decision. It is shown in a diamond shaped box in a flowchart. It will have YES/NO branches to follow. This flowchart has two decision boxes. The first is a selection (IF) statement and asks IF the percentage is greater than or equal to 50. The second one is used to check if the loop has finished or not.
		(iii)	running total within a loop	1	This is one of the three standard algorithms you must recognise. Running total within a loop is used to add up a list of values or update a counter during a series of repetitions.
	c)	(i)	1 mark for each ▶ using loop construct ▶ number of repetitions is classSize	2	You should write your answer in the programming language used during your course, e.g. Python, Java, VB, LiveCode. Line 10 is the start of a loop with Lines 11 to 15 repeating for each testScore in the class. Hint In SQA reference language, using fixed loop: `FOR loop FROM 1 TO classSize DO` Marks could be awarded for using conditional loop which repeats until classSize is reached.
		(ii)	&	1	Concatenation is used to combine two strings or join words and variables into single output message.

Question			Answer	Marks available	Commentary, hints and tips
	d)	(i)	The number of passes equals 9	1	Line 28 produces the output for the program – make sure you use this to structure your answer appropriately. You can use the flowchart or the program to work through with the test data. The possible score is 75 and the program is supposed to count how many people scored over 50% (that would be any testScore 37.5 or more). From the list of test data – 40, 45, 50, 55, 60, 65, 70, 75 and 80 all produce a percentage >=50 hence the answer of 9.
		(ii)	logic error	1	A logic error occurs when the program runs but produces an incorrect or unexpected output. The expected number of passes should have been eight.

		(iii)	1 mark for any one of:
			▸ add input validation to the testScore to prevent entering numbers bigger than possible score
			▸ change condition in Line 13 to
			`IF percentage>=50 AND`
			`percentage<=100 THEN`
				1	The number 80 should not be allowed if the possibleScore for the test is 75. So only eight passes should have been counted.

15	a)		1 mark for each row 	Fields	forename, surname
Tables	Club, Player
Search Criteria	position = "Defenceman" AND town = "Kirkcaldy"	 1 mark for correct fields (with no extras) 1 mark for both table names 1 mark for position="Defenceman" 1 mark for town = "Kirkcaldy"	4	Use the field names exactly as they are given in the tables. Take care on the criteria here as a search for Defencemen (in plural) will find no matches. As this question is about design, it is not necessary to include logical operators (AND) or equi-joins between the tables. You may have answered: position = "Defenceman" AND (club = "Demons" OR club = "Drafters")
	b)		1 mark for each error ▸ age=15 should be age<15 ▸ town="Fife" should be region="Fife" ▸ SELECT playerID, position, age should be SELECT forename, surname, age	2	Read the question carefully to ensure you understand what is being looked for: ▸ names of players – need to include the forename and surname fields in the SELECT clause ▸ Under 15s – not those aged = 15 ▸ Fife players – Fife appears in the region column not the town.

Question			Answer	Marks available	Commentary, hints and tips

	c)		1 mark for each line
			
			`SELECT surname, age`
			`FROM Player`
			`WHERE clubname = "Eddys"`
			`ORDER BY age DESC,`
			`surname ASC;`
				5	Use the SQL command from the previous question to help you structure your answer here.
					
					It is common to get questions at this level with two columns sorted. If you get the first easily enough – age column – then always check to see if there is another column too, because it very probable.
					
					Look at the ages which appear more than once, like 17 and 15 – then check the surnames and you will see they are in alphabetical/ascending order.

	d)		three inputs	1	Inputs are values entered into the program. Here they are: name, year of birth and ticket option. Notice only one ticket option can be selected.
	e)		1 mark each for refinement 5.1 IF currentAge<18 and (ticketcategory is "S" or ticketcategory is "P") then 5.2 discount = 50% 5.3 otherwise if currentAge<18 5.4 discount = 25%	4	You can write your answer using pseudocode, flowchart or structure diagram. You are asked to explain how to get the correct discount for under 18s. As 'S' and 'P' tickets both get 50% discount, it is most efficient to combine both of these criteria together in a single selection statement. As this question asks you to write the design, you can write the discount as the percentage or as a decimal or in words.
16	a)	(i)	polygon	1	A polygon is a two-dimensional shape with any number of straight sides.
		(ii)	1 mark for any one of: ▶ x-coordinate ▶ y-coordinate ▶ line colour	1	A vector graphic is stored as the type of object/shape and a set of properties or attributes to draw it. You are expected to know at least three attributes for different objects.
	b)	(i)	logo.gif	1	It is important to learn the characteristics of gif and jpg so you can decide which version to use.
		(ii)	1 mark for any one of: ▶ gif allows transparency and jpg does not ▶ logo does not have a white background, it is the same as the webpage colour so must be transparent	1	In part a) the logo does not have a grey background. The background must be either white or transparent. If an image with a white background is placed on the grey page, then the white rectangle will show. If it is transparent then the grey page background will show.

Question			Answer	Marks available	Commentary, hints and tips
	c)		1 mark for each ▸ style rules are saved in a CSS document ▸ a link is included in the HTML of each webpage to this CSS file	2	CSS can be applied internally or externally. To apply the same style to lots of pages using internal CSS, it is necessary to copy and paste large sections of code from page to page. If you change style then this needs to be repeated. This answer explains how to apply the same style to lots of pages using external CSS.
	d)	(i)	id selector	1	A CSS selector is used to find (or select) the HTML elements to be formatted. The id selector is used to format HTML elements with id attribute. There cannot be more than one element with the same id. The CSS statement for 'Tour Dates' has the name mainhead and we can see from the screen shot that the styling is only used once on this page, so #mainhead is an id selector.
		(ii)	1 mark for class created with correct structure: dot - name - brackets - semi-colon to separate declarations 1 mark for font-size: 18px 1 mark for color: white	3	`.giglocation{font-size:18px;color:white;}` Each gig has a location, so this styling will be used several times on the page, hence a class selector is required. It is important to use the correct structure for this rule as examples are given in the question of similar rules as a template to follow.
17	a)		1 mark for each ▸ data structure: array ▸ data type: string	2	An array is a list of data items with the same data type. Here the array is a list of names. The names are made up of letters so the data type is string.
	b)	(i)	Colum	1	The code uses a loop to traverse the array. In Line 50 the program compares the winnerName entered with the next item in the array list, and if they are the same then in Line 60, the position in the array is assigned to the variable called winnerPosition. In Line 90, the winnerPosition value is used to update the matching item in the allScores array. As it is the third value in this array that has been updated, then it must have been the third name in the PlayerName array that was entered as the winner in Line 30.

Question			Answer	Marks available	Commentary, hints and tips

		(ii)	1 mark for each
			
			▸ using loop
			▸ repeat for each array element
			▸ displaying allScores array element using loop counter variable
				3	You should write your answer in the programming language used during your course, e.g. Python, Java, VB, LiveCode.
					
					Instead of writing almost exactly the same line of code five times, it is more efficient to use a loop, and use the loop counter variable to access the array elements.
					
					Hint
					
					In SQA reference language:
					`FOR loop FROM 0 TO 4 DO`
					    `SEND allScores[loop] TO DISPLAY`
					`END FOR`

		(iii)	playerName WinnerPosition	1	The names are assigned to the elements of the array called playerName[ ].
	c)		1 mark for any one of: ▸ meaningful variable names ▸ indentation	1	Make sure you read the code given, as only techniques used in the question will be awarded marks. For example, there is no internal commentary so no marks for that technique.
				85	

Practice Paper 2

Section 1

Question			Answer	Marks available	Commentary, hints and tips
1			217	1	<table><tr><td>128</td><td>64</td><td>32</td><td>16</td><td>8</td><td>4</td><td>2</td><td>1</td></tr><tr><td>1</td><td>1</td><td>0</td><td>1</td><td>1</td><td>0</td><td>0</td><td>1</td></tr></table> gives 128 + 64 + 16 + 8 + 1 = 217
2			restricted choice	1	This type of validation is suitable for a field where data has to be selected from a limited list of values – in this case the four season names.
3	a)		27	1	length=3 ^ is the exponential operator So, evaluate 3^3 which is $3 \times 3 \times 3 = 27$
	b)		ALU (arithmetic logic unit)	1	The ALU performs all the calculations.
4			14px	1	The word 'Edinburgh' is part of the body style which is formatted as 14px. Although 'Edinburgh' also has <p> tag there is no styling defined for the <p> element.
5	a)		compiler	1	A compiler translates high-level language instructions into machine code. It does this by going through the source one line at a time and translating it. If there are any syntax errors, it lists them. The object code cannot be run until the whole program is translated.
	b)		syntax error	1	This is an error in the spelling or grammar used when coding.
6	a)		number	1	The meanTempC field contains positive and negative integer numbers.
	b)		<table><tr><td>name</td><td>moons</td></tr><tr><td>Earth</td><td>1</td></tr><tr><td>Mercury</td><td>0</td></tr><tr><td>Moon</td><td>0</td></tr><tr><td>Venus</td><td>0</td></tr></table> 1 mark awarded for correct data values 1 mark awarded for correct sort order	2	Apply the search criteria 'meanTempC>30' to get Mercury, Venus, Earth and Moon. Then apply the first sort order 'moons descending' 1,0,0,0. Then apply the second sort order 'name ascending' to the moons which have the same value. So put the names of the planets with 0 moons in alphabetical order.

Question			Answer	Marks available	Commentary, hints and tips
7			The program is not fit for purpose as the total given is incorrect due to a logic error. 1 mark awarded for correct evaluation 1 mark awarded for appropriate reason	2	The conditional statement in Line 4 is used to count ages above 18 and does not include 18 itself so the total is given as 4 when there are actually five ages in the list eligible to vote.
8			Any two appropriate tests for this code such as: ▶ check the background colour is red ▶ check the heading is centred ▶ check the image is 200px wide by 200px high ▶ test the image called arch is displayed ▶ test the navigation link to the stay.html, eat.html, visit.html, transport.html pages works	2	The answer must relate to the code given. No marks are awarded for generic answers such as 'test the links work'.
9	a)		1 mark for each ▶ correct use of concatenation to combine words and variables ▶ correct text and variable name to form the sentence	2	You should write your answer in the programming language used during your course, e.g. Python, Java, VB, LiveCode. Concatenation is implemented using different operators in each language such as & , +. Hint In SQA reference language: `SEND "The answer is" & answer TO DISPLAY`
	b)		Execution error	1	An execution error occurs while the program is running. The test data given results in trying to divide by zero.
10			1 mark for any one of: ▶ process data lawfully, fairly and in a transparent manner in relation to individuals ▶ data must be used for the declared purpose only ▶ limit the data needed for the declared purpose ▶ store accurate data ▶ hold data securely	1	Describe one of the implications of GDPR to the school as they are storing personal data.
11	a)		register	1	It is common to have questions about basic computer architecture components. In this case, reference is made to the 'lives' variable used in the code.
	b)		address bus	1	
	c)		data bus	1	
12	a)		flowchart	1	A flowchart shows the order of execution of instructions from the start at the top to the end at the bottom.

Question			Answer	Marks available	Commentary, hints and tips
	b)		1 mark for any one of: ▸ Household = 1? ▸ Option = 10? ▸ Option = 12?	1	A conditional statement is used to make a decision. In a flowchart, a decision is shown in a ◇ box which contains a question about some data from the program. Branches coming from this should be labelled to show which branch is taken for each possible answer to the question.
	c)	(i)	£90	1	Use the data given in the question to follow the steps in the flowchart: bill = £1200 number in household = 1 (single person) so follow the 'yes' branch to work out discounted bill (25% discount on £1200 = £900) payment option = 10 months so follow the 'yes' branch to work out monthly payment (900 divided by 10).
		(ii)	£200	1	Use the data given in the question to follow the steps in the flowchart: bill = £2400 number in household>1 (large household) so follow the 'no' branch payment option = 12 months so follow the 'yes' branch to work out monthly payment (2400 divided by 12).
				25	

Section 2

Question			Answer	Marks available	Commentary, hints and tips
13	a)		pseudocode	1	Pseudocode is a method of designing a program that uses a language that is halfway between ordinary language and programming code. The main algorithm is written and then refinements give more detail for each step of the algorithm.
	b)		assignment	1	Assignment is the programming construct used to put a value into a variable. It is written in the exam paper like this: `SET variable TO <a value>` or `SET variable TO <an expression>` Assignment can be used to: ▸ declare an initial value ▸ store a value entered at the keyboard in a variable ▸ store the result of calculation ▸ update a value already held in a variable.
	c)	i)	string	1	The stem of the question tells you that a registration plate is made up of characters. The diagram shows you an example in case you don't know what one looks like. A string data type is used to hold a sequence of characters.
		ii)	Boolean	1	Step 2.3 tells you that the badge requirement is True or False. A Boolean data type can only be True or false.
	d)		input validation	1	This is one of the three standard algorithms you must recognise. Input validation is required to check that values entered are sensible or within acceptable limits. Step 2.2 indicates that only 1 or 2 should be entered for this input. Any other input is not allowed, and an error message should be displayed to the user.
	e)		function: length parameter: registration	2	Predefined functions are pieces of code that carry out an operation and return the value to your program. A parameter is the value passed to the function for it to work with. In Step 3.1 the number of characters in the registration has to be found. The length function works this out by using the registration number entered by the user.

Question			Answer	Marks available	Commentary, hints and tips
	f)		1 mark for each ▶ number of characters * characterPrice ▶ adding badgePrice ▶ multiplying total by number of plates required ▶ assigning cost to a suitable variable	4	You can write your answer using pseudocode, flowchart or structure diagram. It is possible to write a single calculation, but you will still get marks if you write it separately. Possible answer 1: cost for one plate is (number of characters * characterPrice) + badgePrice total cost is cost for one plate * number of plates Possible answer 2: cost is ((number of characters * characterPrice) + badgePrice) * number of plates
	g)		£40	1	Use the data from the code and the question to work through each step: characterPrice = 2.50 badgePrice = 0 registration = XYZ123 number of plates = 2 badge requirement = True number of characters in registration = 6 badgePrice updated to 5 cost is ((6*2.50)+5)*2=£40
14	a)	(i)	range check	1	A range check is used to ensure that data entered into the field must be between a maximum and minimum limit.
		(ii)	presence check	1	A presence check is used to ensure that the field must have data entered for every record.
	b)		<table><tr><td>Field(s)</td><td>employeeName, timeTaken</td></tr><tr><td>Table(s)</td><td>TeamMember, Activity</td></tr><tr><td>Search Criteria</td><td>age>40 AND distance=10 AND type= "Run"</td></tr><tr><td>Sort Order</td><td>timeTaken ascending</td></tr></table> 1 mark for correct fields (with no extras) and both table names 1 mark for correct sort order 1 mark for age>40 1 mark for distance = 10 1 mark for type= "Run"	5	Use the field names exactly as they are given in the tables. As this question is about design, it is not necessary to include logical operators (AND) or equi-joins between the tables
	c)	(i)	Boolean	1	A Boolean data type can only be True or false. It is often represented by a check/tick box.

Question			Answer	Marks available	Commentary, hints and tips
		(ii)	`INSERT INTO Activity VALUES(6, "Cycle", "5/4/2020", 44.27, 20, 104)`	2	Use the example given to help get the correct structure for your answer. Text values need to be inside quotes. Make sure you arrange the data items in the correct order for the field in the table.
		(iii)	referential integrity	1	employeeID in the Activity table is a foreign key linked to the primary key employeeID in the TeamMember table. Referential integrity means that the data held in the foreign key field must refer to an entry in the primary key field of the linked table. Referential integrity stops a record being added to the Activity table if it is not linked to a record in the TeamMember table. In other words, you should not be able to add activity details for someone who does not exist in the TeamMember table.
15	a)		Any two from: ▶ helps clarify the design of each webpage ▶ helps identify the features to be implemented on the website ▶ can be used to help evaluate whether the system is fit for purpose after development is complete	2	This question is about the reason for analysis rather than actually carrying out analysis to identify end-user needs. It is important to know the reasons for identifying end-user requirements.
	b)		1 mark for any one of: ▶ gives potential end users of the finished product an indication of how the product will look ▶ allows navigation structure to be tested ▶ confirm the position of page objects are acceptable to the user	1	A low-fidelity prototype is a paper-based version of the website, drawn on paper or card with pens. They include text and images that are planned to appear on the finished webpages and areas for user interaction. It is important to know what a low-fidelity prototype is as well as why it is used.
	c)	(i)	1 mark for type of object/shape 1 mark for either of: ▶ Stored as a set of definitions/properties/instructions/attributes ▶ Example of at least two attributes	2	Vector graphics are made up of shapes like rectangle, ellipse, line, polygon – in some questions in SQA papers it is these shapes or objects that you have to identify. The objects themselves are not stored, but the attributes to create the shapes such as coordinates, fill colour, line colour.
		(ii)	gif	1	Animation is only possible with gif file format. The other graphic formats – jpg and png – do not allow for animation.
	d)	(i)	96 kHz	1	The higher the sampling rate, the higher the quality of the sound.

Question			Answer	Marks available	Commentary, hints and tips
		(ii)	Larger file size	1	With the higher sampling rate, more samples are being stored so the file size is bigger.
	e)	(i)	relative	1	Both the workout.html and home.html pages being linked are stored within the same website on the same server. A relative address only needs to contain the path to a page being linked to on the same server (whereas an absolute address needs to include all information needed for the browser to locate the file, including the server address).
		(ii)	1 mark for indication of folder one level above the current folder: ../ 1 mark for correct path: media/ video/ 1 mark for video file name: squats. mp4	3	../media/videos/squats.mp4 The workout.html page containing this code is located in the pages folder. To locate the video file required, it is necessary to go up one level back to the root folder (../), then follow the path through the media folder to the video folder (media/video/) to reach the file (squats.mp4)
		(iii)	Less time taken to transfer files to the end user.	1	Compression will reduce the size of the file, but this is not a benefit in itself to the end user. Because the file size is smaller, it will download faster.
	f)		1 mark for id created with correct structure: hash - name - brackets - semi-colon to separate declarations 1 mark for text-align:center 1 mark for font-size:16px (or larger) 1 mark for color:yellow	4	`#mainheading{text-align: center; font-size: 20px; color: yellow;}` It is important to use the correct structure for this rule as examples are given in the question of similar rules as a template to follow.
16	a)		1 mark for inputs: parking bay number, car registration, length of stay 1 mark for output: amount to be charged	2	Inputs are values required by the program and are often entered by the user. Outputs are values produced by the program after processing and often displayed on the screen.
	b)	(i)	real	1	The cost per minute for tariff A is shown in the diagram as 0.0215884 – a number with a decimal part. This will need to be stored as a real number. Although the programming language you have used may refer to a real data type as SINGLE, DOUBLE or FLOAT, in the exam you should use real.
		(ii)	integer	1	The number of minutes to stay is referenced in the Duration column of the diagram as 'each minute' indicating whole minutes will be charged for. Whole numbers with no decimal part are known as integers.

Question			Answer	Marks available	Commentary, hints and tips
		(iii)	mantissa: 21584 exponent: −1	2	The mantissa is the part of a number located after a decimal point and the exponent is used to show where the point should be placed.
	c)		1 mark for each ▶ ending loop ▶ minutes >= 1 and minutes <= 240	2	You should write your answer in the programming language used during your course, e.g. Python, Java, VB, LiveCode. This is an example of the standard algorithm for input validation. Charging starts at 1 minute and the maximum stay is 4 hours (240 minutes). One possible solution is: `UNTIL minutes >= 1 and minutes <= 240` Some programming languages use a WHILE loop so marks would also be given for WHILE minutes<1 OR minutes>240.
	d)	(i)	1 mark for each ▶ calculating first 30 minutes on tariff A (costA * 30) ▶ calculating cost of tariff B minutes (minute – 30 * costB) ▶ calculating total cost by adding the two above ▶ basic calculation stored	4	You should write your answer in the programming language used during your course, e.g. Python, Java, VB, LiveCode. Hint `SET parkingcharge TO (costA * 30)+((minutes - 30) * costB)`
		(ii)	1 mark for each ▶ Function: round ▶ Parameters: parkingcharge OR 2	2	Predefined functions carry out an operation and return the value to your program. A parameter is the value passed to the function for it to work with. In Line 41, the parking charge has to be displayed to 2 decimal places. The round function carries out this task. The round function needs two parameters – the variable to be rounded (parkingcharge) and the number of decimal places to round off to (2).
	e)		1 mark for any one of: ▶ worked out the exit time ▶ worked out the current date	1	A process is something that the program does. In this case, two inputs (car reg and parking bay number) are displayed as well as the parking charge. So, consider how the program got the other items which are shown.
17	a)		1 mark for div formatting ▶ size of text: 20px ▶ colour of text: white 1 mark for class .section formatting ▶ background colour: DarkBlue ▶ aligned: center	2	HTML code shows the 'Down on the Farm' as a <div> element so the CSS for div applies. The div also has a class="section" attribute so the CSS for .section applies.

Question			Answer	Marks available	Commentary, hints and tips
	b)		Any two from: ▶ The id of an HTML element is unique within a page, so the id selector is used to select one unique element to format ▶ whereas the class of an HTML document can be used by many elements on a page so the class selector selects several elements with the same class attribute to format ▶ class selector written with .name whereas id selector written with #name	2	A CSS selector is used to find (or select) the HTML elements to be formatted. The class selector is used to format HTML elements with a class attribute. Many HTML elements can share the same class so a single CSS can be used to style many elements in the same way. The id selector is used to format HTML elements with id attribute. There cannot be more than one element with the same id.
	c)	(i)	JavaScript	1	JavaScript is the scripting language that can be used to create and manipulate HTML elements.
		(ii)	1 mark for each ▶ load the page and check the words 'Here are the latest arrivals' are formatted as white text on red background ▶ position pointer over the words and check the lettering has changed to blue	2	It is necessary to explain how the testing is done to ensure the JavaScript works properly. You need to say more than 'check it changes to blue'. The text is part of the div section with id="activities" so when the page is first opened in the browser the #activities formatting is applied. The JavaScript event is what happens to an HTML element – in this case the text turns blue when the cursor is moved over it.
	d)		jpg	1	The image is referenced in the <img> element. The image file is piglet.jpg so the file name is 'piglets' and the file format is .jpg.

	e)		1 mark for each
			
			▶ adding <ul> and </ul> to open and close unordered bullet list
			
			▶ changing <p> and </p> tags to <li> and </li> tags
				2	`<ul>`
					`<li> Visit the stables </li>`
					`<li> Feed the chickens</li>`
					`<li> Take a tractor ride</li>`
					`</ul>`
					
					Remember that <ul> produces a bullet list while <ol> produces a numbered list.
					
					Each list item needs <li> to start and </li> to end.

	f)		1 mark for creating selector with correct structure: a - brackets - semi-colon to end declaration 1 mark for color: yellow;	2	`a {color: yellow;}` Links are written as <a> elements so create a CSS rule for the <a> selector. It is important to use the correct structure for this rule as examples are given in the question of similar rules as a template to follow.

Question			Answer	Marks available	Commentary, hints and tips
	g)		1 mark for any one of: ▸ checking the website meets the end-user requirements determined at the analysis phase ▸ checking the website meets the functional requirements determined at the analysis phase	1	To evaluate a website to see if it is fit for purpose, it is necessary to review what the expectations were for the website. These expectations and requirements are agreed at the analysis stage. During evaluation, the requirements should be checked off and tested.
18	a)		1 mark for primary keys 1 mark for foreign key <table><tr><td>Entity</td><td>Primary Key</td><td>Foreign Key</td></tr><tr><td>Job</td><td>jobID</td><td>account Number</td></tr><tr><td>Account</td><td>account Number</td><td></td></tr></table>	2	The primary key is used to uniquely identify each record in an entity. In the job entity, each jobID is unique In the Account entity, each account is identified by its accountNumber. The foreign key is a primary key value form another table, used to link table together. Here each job is linked to an account by the accountNumber.
	b)		1 mark for 1:M relationship MANY Jobs are done on ONE account **or** ONE account has MANY jobs	1	A one-to-many relationship exists when one record in one table can be linked to many records in another table, but one record in the second table can be linked to only one record in the first table. In this question, one account can get lots of jobs done but one jobID is linked to only one account.
	c)		1 mark for each ▸ field length validation check ▸ value for accountNumber used in the INSERT command must not meet the criteria of seven digits	2	A validation check is set to ensure that the account number has got seven digits. This is called a field length check. The error will occur if the incorrect data is entered.
	d)	(i)	The end user wanted to get a list of (1 mark each): ▸ company names and dates ▸ who got a service done	2	The end-user requirement refers to what the end user wanted to achieve by running the SQL command.

		(ii)	1 mark for each line
			```SELECT jobID, company,```
			``` contact```
			```FROM Account, Job```
			```WHERE Account.accountNumber```
			``` = Job.accountNumber```
			```AND priority = True```
			```AND cost<100;```
				5	It can be helpful to read the question and highlight the criteria to be found and fields to be displayed.
					Use the SQL command from the previous question to help you structure your answer here.

	e)	(i)	This SQL statement will update all the records where the priority status is currently False.	1	Records are updated based on matching the criteria given in the WHERE clause. So, any record that contains False in the priority filed will be updated to True – that is the records for CJ Kelly and Quinn Ltd and not just CJ Kelly.

Question			Answer	Marks available	Commentary, hints and tips

		(ii)	1 mark for correct WHERE clause
			
			`WHERE accountNumber = 4355326;`
			
			or
			
			`WHERE company = "CJ Kelly";`
				1	To correct the SQL, it is necessary to match the correct account in the WHERE clause. This should be done using the accountNumber as this is the unique identifier, but it could also be done using the company name with this limited set of data.

	f)		1 mark for any of: ▶ check the results produced are accurate ▶ check fit for purpose by ensuring it carries out all the functional requirements	1	To evaluate a database it is necessary to review what the expectations were for the database – what queries was it expected to be able to deal with. If it can do these and produce accurate results then it is fit for purpose.
	g)		Any two from: ▶ reduce monitor settings ▶ set computers to go into sleep mode after a period of inactivity ▶ activate hard disk shut down settings	2	It is necessary to know how the impact on the environment of using computers can be reduced.
				85	